Rib

Speaks

An Anthology of Poems and Short Stories for Men and Women

Keshia L. Spencer

The Rib Speaks
by Keshia L. Spencer
Published by 3rd Dimension Publishing
PO Box 38
Monmouth Junction, NJ 08852
www.3rdddimensionpublishing.com

© Keshia L. Spencer
Contact the author:
Website: **www.theribspeaks.com**
Email: **Keshia@theribspeaks.com**
        keshyasp@yahoo.com

ISBN – 10 09746567-2-0
ISBN – 13 9780974656724

Library of Congress Cataloging -in-Publication Data

Christian Living/Poetry

Spencer, Keshia L.

This God-given project is dedicated to Daddy and Jackie.
Thanks for your applause from heaven.

To my mother, your support has been my anchor for as long
as I can remember.

To Sis Kidd
(Ola)
Thanks for
your love,
Keshia

Acknowledgments

First and foremost, I must give thanks to the only true and living God. You allowed me to live long enough to see Your favor and blessings upon my life. Your inspiration and divine guidance enabled me to complete this project and I attribute all of my success to You.

To my father, Elmo Spencer, and sister, Jackie Spencer, you are now with the Lord. I can imagine Daddy playing his harmonica and Jackie singing along. Our lost was heaven's gain and I can't wait to see you again. Your legacy continues on earth and you will never be forgotten. To my mother, Joyce Spencer, you kept asking me, "When are you going to finish your book?" This question pushed me closer and closer to publication. I did it!

To my family, friends, and everyone who supported this project by buying this book, I pray that you will receive 100 percent of all the good that you bestow upon others.

What a mighty God we serve! He makes all things possible and does all things well. Thank You Lord for calling me Your own.

Table of Contents

Introduction

So often we pick up a pen and piece of paper without fully knowing the purpose of these tools. It could be to compose words to a song, draw a picture on canvas, or draft a letter to the one we love. After the initial uncertainties and repeated efforts, a finished product is created. At this point, we then conclude that what sits before us was always meant to be.

Daily, thoughts would race through my mind: thoughts about life, thoughts about God, and even thoughts about His love. Each thought competed for an opportunity to be expressed on paper so I decided to give them justice. I took a pad and pencil and refused to let them go until something legible had been produced.

The result was this book, an anthology of poems and short stories about various topics and practical life lessons. Included are poems about praise, Bible truths, family and even faith. My short stories are encouraging and entertaining as they highlight some pertinent issues vital to our everyday existence. I'll also discuss what it means to be a woman, the prestigious honor of being a man, and how the Lord will always provide. Adam came from God, Eve came from Adam, and her legacy continues through me (Genesis 2:22). As a mouthpiece of inspiration and hope, I present unto you,

The Rib Speaks:
An Anthology of Poems and Short Stories for Men and Women

I.

Let's

Talk

About

Praise!

Unrestrained Expression

Growing up I was often taught the importance of exercising restraint and doing things in moderation. These concepts depict order and acceptable social behavior and should serve as guides throughout my entire life. I agree that this is sound advice and something to which I should always subscribe. But what am I supposed to do when it comes to praise? Am I supposed to be obsessed with order and moderation? Should I be more concerned about how I appear to others rather than how I look to God? Or should I be willing to engage in the rigorous activity and public display of praise even at the expense of my own reputation?

I choose to do the latter. When it comes to praise, restraint and moderation are not even options. You see, I know the Savior personally. And when I recall to mind who He is and all that He has done, it's rather difficult for me to maintain order and acceptable social behavior as determined by the world. I must clap my hands and shout real loud because God is worthy to be praised. To Him I must pay homage, honor and glory because He continues to make ways for His people. Unrestrained expression is my mode of praise as I lift up the Name of the Lord.

Without turning to the Hebrew or Greek immediately, let's look in the English dictionary and consider the meaning of praise. Praise denotes an expression of approval, commendation, or admiration. It also means to extol or exalt a deity, ruler, or hero. Based on my experience, praise is a public display of gratitude where the focus is God and He is showered with high accolades. You can praise a child for getting straight As in school. You can commend a chef for making a scrumptious meal. You can even admire an entertainer for a job well-done. But on a more elevated scale, I want to talk about praising the Lord. He's not one of several deities, but the only true and living God. Even His name is great and according to Psalm 72:17a, *It* endures forever. We are to lift our voices along with a bodily demonstration of thanks because God alone made the heavens and the earth and there is none like Him.

The Hebrew word for praise is halal. It means to make a show, to boast, clamor foolishly, glory, rave, or be as mad. It is a loud sustained noise that involves shouting, clapping, dancing and playing of musical instruments. While we offer thanks, words like, "Lord, I love You, You are worthy, and I'm nothing without You!" fill the atmosphere. We know where our help comes from and in whom we can depend. So praise must include an acknowledgment of Who God is and all that He has done. We may not always agree with what He chooses for us, but we must reverence His faithfulness. Even when we think He's moving too slow we must admit that He is the God of perfect timing. In any event, praise is always appropriate because He is the Author and Finisher of our faith and above Him there is no other.

In Genesis 22:14, Abraham praised God for being Jehovah-Jireh. God does provide and tends to everything that concerns His people. Gideon acknowledged Him as Jehovah-Shalom because He is peace (Judges 6:24). In Exodus 17:15, Moses worshipped God as Jehovah-Nissi, our banner and reigning victory. Today, we honor Him as the King of kings, Lord of lords, and the fact that He reigns forever.

Although God requires order, praise won't work for you if you're trying to be sophisticated. Check out David in II Samuel 6:14. He danced before the Lord with all his might so much so that he came clean out of his cloak. His wife, Michal, didn't appreciate his behavior because to her it was inappropriate for a king. She considered David as behaving unseemly and was thoroughly embarrassed. Excuse my poor grammar, but his response to her was, "If you think this is bad, you ain't seen nothin' yet. I will get even MORE wilder than this, causing you much more contempt." (II Samuel 6:21-22) David was determined to give God the praise despite what anyone thought and how he looked. I don't know about you, but I am a modern-day David. This means that I have made an unrelenting commitment to bless the Lord at all times and His praises will always be in my mouth (Psalm 34:1).

Even though God is the focus, praise won't work for you if you have a fear of being seen. It is a public display that involves singing (Psalm 149:1), dancing (Psalm 149:3), clapping and lifting of the hands (Psalm 47:1 and 134:2). If you can't tolerate noise or loud music, praise will definitely be unbearable. Psalm 150 involves all the musical instruments and Psalm 100:1 commands us to make a joyful noise all across the land.

I have learned to praise Him through adverse circumstances, questionable events, and different levels of uncertainties. I most certainly praise Him when things are going well, as my needs are being met, and when He grants my desires. Praise is my weapon that silences the enemy and sets things in order. Praise precedes miracles; it welcomes God and gives Him a place of habitation in the midst of His people. Praise is His rightful due as He gives us power to defeat the devil and live a victorious life. Praise is what He deserves as He validates our existence and gives us a reason to live. Praise is always appropriate because like I said He is the King of kings, Lord of lords, and Only Potentate (I Timothy 6:15). So don't hold back. Give Him what He deserves. Let the world know that you are not ashamed and as long as you have breath, you will give Him the praise (Psalm 150:6).

The following poems are lyrical expressions of praise. Please join me as I lift up the Name of the Lord.

Psalm 150

Everything that has breath
Must praise the Lord
The animals, the trees
The waters and breeze.

Everything that has life
Must praise the Lord
Man, woman, and child
Tamed beasts and wild.

Everything in creation
Must praise the mighty God
He made everything
So let the praises ring!

Lift your voice
And shout real loud
Here below
And beyond the clouds.

Clap your hands
As well as sing
I vow to do
This very thing.

The heavens and earth
All make a sound
The trumpet and cymbal
And those around.

The timbrel and dance
The psaltery and harp
Unite as one
To do their part.

These instruments
Join in together
To cease in praise
They will never.

The sound is high
The effect is sure
In the temple
Lord, we adore.

We bow to Thee
O mighty King
In You we live
And have our being.

I'll never cease
To give You praise
Like David I'll bless You
All my days.

Praise Him!!!

Praise Him for
His wonder and deeds
His excellent greatness
And meeting your needs.

The firmament of
His mighty power
The organs, the strings
And heavenly choir.

The cherubim and seraphim
Hide their face in fear
They reverence God's presence
And having Him so near.

Even the angels
Sing a pleasant tune
They fly to and fro
Above the stars and moon.

But still no one
Can praise Him for me
A rock crying out
Will never be.

I will lift
Real loud my voice
Not by force
But by choice.

I know that praise
Is comely for the saints
In the Holy of Holies
And beyond the gates.

I love to praise Him
Both night and day
His radiant glory
Shows me the way.

The Awesomeness of God

I often sit and wonder
Contemplate and ponder.

At God's masterful creation
Forming the races and the nations.

Kings and queens must bow to Thee
Across the earth, both land and sea.

In the end all must confess
Jesus as Lord and nothing less.

He is the Great I Am
Jehovah-Jireh is His Name.

The Father of us all
The Only Potentate He is called.

Sovereign Ruler and Royalty
He died and rose with victory.

The earth is adorned with His glory
As she tells her own worship story.

Still I sit and look in awe
Feeling His presence both near and far.

God is awesome and I must mention
Heaven and earth are His rendition.

Join With Creation

Sitting by the waters
I heard nature sing a lovely tune
Even the air transferred
The presence of the Lord.

The flowers emitted
A fresh and lovely fragrance
The birds joined in
As the trees clapped their hands.

The dove is gentle
As she soars in adoration
To honor her Maker
As He constantly provides.

The grass is so green
Beyond the color of new money
The animals declare
God's strength and mighty power.

Even the sun is radiant
And the moon has a role, too
They along with the stars
Continue to light my path.

Then God made man
In His likeness and His image
The crowning achievement
Of His creative work.

Therefore, we must bow
And join with creation
To acknowledge Who God is
And all that He has done.

II.

Biblical

Truths

It is finished!

A few years ago, I preached a message entitled, *It is Finished*. This statement conveys one of the most profound truths revered in Christendom. It declares that Jesus completed everything necessary in order for us to obtain salvation. His mission was accomplished and thoroughly complete. We no longer have to offer the blood of goats and bulls because such sacrifices are not sufficient. In the Old Testament, they only covered sin. But in the New Testament, the blood of Jesus took away sin and no other sacrifices are required.

Jesus was born to die, not for anything that He had done, but for the sins of the world. He was born to suffer and bear many stripes, not for any sickness of His own, but for the healing of the nations. He was crucified, but on the third day He rose with all power in His hands. This gave us victory over death and the free gift of eternal life. It is finished! Let these words marinade in your spirit as we briefly review some of the accomplishments of Calvary.

I'll begin with the miracle of healing. Although doctors are instrumental in our well-being, complete healing comes only through Jesus. As a result of the beatings and stripes that He endured, we can be whole in our spirit, soul, and body. I Peter 2:24 declares that by His stripes we were healed. And Malachi 4: 2 states that the Son of righteousness has come with healing in His wings. It is finished assures believers that Jesus is the Master Physician and He has the final say despite what the medical report conveys.

Salvation was also finished on Calvary. What I like about the plan of salvation is that it is all inclusive. Romans 10:13 specifically says, *whosoever*. Whosoever means that anyone can call on the Name of the Lord and be saved. If you're male or female, black or white, short or tall, Jesus died for your sins.

All you have to do is adhere to Romans 10: 9 - 10. Confess Jesus as Lord, believe in your heart that God raised Him from the dead, and you will be saved.

As a result of Calvary, deliverance is finished. You no longer have to be enslaved by demonic forces and the perils of darkness. God will bring you into the marvelous light of liberty and you can enjoy the abundant life that He desires for us all. Jesus' mission included deliverance to the captives and freedom to those who are mentally or emotionally bruised (Luke 4:18 and 19). Refuse to be imprisoned by defeat and choose rather to enjoy the privileges made possible by our Lord.

Finally, let's talk about the rapture. Today you don't hear too much about this topic. This is partly due to the prosperity and get rich quick messages that have taken precedence. The other reason is that we can get so caught up in the here and now that we forget that Jesus is coming again. The message of Calvary includes the rapture and the fact that we must be ready. When I was coming up in the Pentecostal church we were what I would call *rapture conscious*. The leaders put so much fear in us that we thought Jesus was coming at any minute. Although they were a bit legalistic, we knew that we were pilgrims passing through and this was not our home. Without being doctrinal or legalistic myself, I simply want to remind you that Jesus is coming again. The rapture is the hope of the Church and we look forward to being caught up to meet the Lord in the air. We will then reign with Him forever more in our heavenly abode (I Thessalonians 4:13-18).

Wow! Did you realize that so much was accomplished on Calvary? And I only told you part of the story I am so glad Jesus died on the cross and rose from the dead. I'm equally excited about the words of the song which says,

We don't have to kill the Lamb anymore
We don't have to sprinkle the blood on the door
God has provided in place of the lamb
He is the Great I AM.

Enjoy all that God has made available for you through His Son. Jesus set out to save the world from the curse of sin and destroy the works of the enemy. He didn't leave anything undone which give us all the right to declare,

IT IS FINISHED!!!

The following poems are a collection of other biblical truths. While reading them keep in mind that man cannot live by bread alone, but by every word that proceeds from the mouth of God shall man live (Matthew 4:4).

It's in God's Word

It's in God's Word
What He can do
And each page reveals
Who He is.

So let's review
True accounts
Of His sovereignty
And miraculous power.

He fed over 5,000
Walked on water
Parted the Red Sea
And sent manna from heaven.

He alone
Was Israel's army
Giving Pharaoh
An unexpected end.

Jonah was in a whale
For three whole days
When Moses struck the rock
A divine liquid gushed out.

Job received double
For all his trouble
And David could do nothing
But bless God's holy Name.

It's in God's Word
That we must live
By what proceeds
From His mouth.

It's in God's Word
That He doesn't change
The same yesterday
And forevermore.

God promised never
To leave us alone
As our heavenly Father
He watches over us.

It's in God's Word
And by it we live
Forever to honor
It in our hearts.

Salvation is Free

Come if you
Have no money
To a land flowing
With milk and honey.

Come if you
Are void of peace
His love for you
Will never cease.

Come He is
The Righteous Judge
For your sins
He'll hold no grudge.

Come receive
Joy in full
From your sins
You He'll pull.

Come as you are
And from this day
Eternal life
Will be your pay.

Come if you're thirsty
And need to eat
In God there is
No defeat.

Don't be fooled
By Satan's illusion
He offers only
A strong delusion.

Don't be fooled
By worldly riches
Adhere to what
The Bible teaches.

Be satisfied
God offers bread
Delight yourself
Be spiritually fed.

On the cross
He paid the price
Our Savior and Lord
Jesus Christ!

Isaiah said,
Incline your ear
You shall live
If you will hear.*

Salvation is free
God's Spirit is flowing
A process of reaping,
Gathering and sowing.

The mercy of God
Is sound and sure
His covenant with man
Will always endure.

Salvation is free
And has no cost
Confess Him as Lord
And suffer no loss.

*Isaiah 55:3

What Does it Mean to be Delivered?

What does it mean to be delivered?
What does it mean to be set free?
What does it mean to be delivered?
What does it mean for you and me?

It means to walk
By faith and not by sight
Trusting God
With all your might.

It means for God
To dig down deep
Giving you all
That you need.

It means for Him
To renew your mind
And thoughts of Christ
You will find.

Deliverance is
God's mighty Hand
Intervening
On behalf of man.

I'm glad He chose
To snatch me out
No more destruction
I've changed my route.

I know what it means
To be delivered
It's in my desert
Having many rivers.

It means in God
To be set free
Receiving all
He has for me.

Deliverance is
God's holy power
Available for you
This very hour.

Speak it into
The atmosphere
What you pray
God will hear.

He will meet you
Where you are
Hasn't He proven
Himself so far?

I know what it means to be delivered?
I know what it means to be set free?
I know what it means to be delivered?
I know what it means for you and me?

It means refusing
The bondage of sin
And living so
You'll live again.

So don't give up
In midstream
Your reward is like
You've never seen.

What a Man

"What manner of man is this that even the wind and the sea obey him?"
Mark 4:41

There once was a Man
Who walked the earth
Many overlooked
What He was worth.

He calmed the sea
5,000 He fed
He healed the sick
And raised the dead.

God and human
At the same time
Releasing us
From Satan's bind.

Born of Mary
And Joseph, too
Worship is
His rightful due.

Jesus Christ
Is His Name
Forever He
Remains the same.

Just confess Him
As Lord and King
Eternal life
This will bring.

What a Man He was
Crucified on a hill
Delighting to do
His Father's will.

He gave His life
For humanity
Taking on sin
So we'd be free.

What a Man Who gave
All that He had
Satan is furious
And extremely mad.

He is now
A defeated foe
In Jesus' Name
You must go.

Forever God lives
His love is everywhere
When you call Him
He'll be there.

Because He promised
Never to leave
On these words
We can cleave.

What a Man Who made
The seas obey
In truth He reigns
And leads the way.

The Rapture

"Surely, I come quickly. Amen..." Revelations 22:20

Jesus promised
That He would return
His second appearance
Is what the Church yearns.

The rapture itself
Will be carefully orchestrated
Lend me your ear
As God's Word demonstrates it.

The archangel will blow
And the trumpet will sound
In the grave
The saints won't be bound.

The Lord Himself
Will descend from heaven
Those sleep in the Lord
Will also be with Him.

The dead in Christ
Will first arise
Then we who remain
Will meet in the skies.

Leaving the earth
We'll be caught up
Destined for heaven
Not Satan's rut.

The sinners behind
Must endure tribulation
If you're not clear
Then read Revelation.

The coming of the Lord
Is like a thief in the night
First peace and safety
Then destruction forthright.

When the saints disappear
The world will be amazed
At our sudden departure
Up above they will gaze.

The media will call it
A great catastrophe
But the saints will know it
As our final victory.

I can't wait to inhabit
My mansion in the sky
Streets of pure gold
We'll walk, both you and I.

Comfort one another
With these words
Forever we'll reign
And be with the Lord.

The Fall of Satan

"I beheld Satan as lightning fall from heaven." Luke 10:18

Satan has fallen
From God's heavenly sky
What a fool you were
To rebel on high.*

God is the smarter
Ever wise is He
Satan, no glory
Belongs to thee.

You have no power
You only make a noise
Unlike a roaring lion
You have no real poise.

At one time you were beauty
Covered with many precious stones
Then pride deceived you
And you weren't alone.

A third of the angels fell
With you as their master
All doomed for hell
And eternal disaster.

Your imps and demonic spirits
Travel to and fro
In the Name of Jesus
Satan, you must go.

The saints have the power
In God's holy Name
To tread upon serpents
Like Christ, we're the same.

Don't forget your armor
And always plead the blood
So you won't be consumed
And overtaken like the Flood*.

We do have power
And authority
While not forsaking
Humility.

Don't let pride
Cause you to fall
Submit to Jesus
And you'll stand tall.

The fall of Satan
Is a valuable lesson
Resist what he offers
Receive God's blessings!

*Isaiah 14: 12-15; Genesis 7:1-12

That's Love

"Greater love hath no man than this, that a man would lay down his life for his friends." John 15:13

Pierced in His side
For our sins He died
Freely gave his life
Not in anger or in strife…
That's Love!

He left His throne of glory
We yet tell the story
A great sacrifice He gave
So that we could be saved…
That's Love!

He took many stripes for our healing
With no regrets, neither unwilling
His body He did give
So that you and I could live…
Oh, that's Love!

He spoke no guile
And had no sin
What He promised
We can depend.

Just like He said
The third day He rose
This is the way
That God chose.

They ran and then
Rolled back the stone
Just like He said
He was gone.

"Why seek ye the living
Amongst the dead?"*
Go ahead, Gabriel
Very well said.

What I like about God
Is that He always has a plan
Although Jesus left
He is coming again.

On the right hand of the Father
He has all authority
Because of Jesus Christ
We'll live eternally…

Oh, that's Love!

*Luke 24:5

III.

God

Will

Provide

First Things First

Have you ever wondered what it means to put God first? Does it mean to have a robotic existence forsaking your own dreams and aspirations? Or is God simply asking you to relax, make Him your priority, and trust Him for your daily provisions?

The latter is correct. God desires to have the pre-eminence in your life while at the same time He respects your own individual will. By giving Him the pre-eminence, this means that He is your priority and you're willing to work in conjunction with His plans. In addition, God doesn't want you to be worried today about tomorrow because He has everything under control. He also wants you to know that you mean more to Him than the lilies of the field and the fowl of the air. Therefore, you must seek Him and His kingdom *first* knowing that everything else will be added (Matthew 6:33).

From time to time God has to remind us to put Him first. We have so much going on in our lives that it's easy to lose track of the Source. Day to day concerns, anxiety, and even fear tempts us to lose hope. This is why we must take comfort in knowing that God will not forsake His people. He didn't just leave us here to fend for ourselves. Just like He feeds the birds and clothes the grass, on a larger scale He will take care of us.

So try not to worry. Don't let the cares of life take you on an emotional frenzy. And don't act in haste just because things are not lined up exactly the way you want. In due time, your plans and purpose will be fulfilled. And your dreams and aspirations will come to pass. Your life is worth more than food and your body is worth more than raiment.

So seek God first and all that you need will be added unto you.

Some of you are wondering, "Well, how do I put God first?" Here are some suggestions:

1. Meet God daily in prayer. Luke 18:1 instructs us to always pray so that we won't faint or lose heart. We must be in constant communion with the Lord so that He can reveal His will and His ways. Your prayer time should not be a complaining session. Instead, it should be a combination of praise, worship, and thanksgiving. It should also include making your requests, stating your desires, and even praying for someone else.

2. Fasting is another way to put God first. The privilege of natural food is replaced by the pleasure of spiritual food. This includes feasting on the Word of God while basking in His holy presence. Fasting also allows your spiritual and physical strength to be renewed (Isaiah 58).

3. Honoring God with the first fruits of all your increase constitutes putting Him first (Proverbs 3:9, 10 & Malachi 3:10-12). He gives us the power to make wealth. Therefore, we must worship Him with our tithes and offerings.

4. Finally, you should put God first when it comes to relationships. If you acknowledge Him, He will definitely direct you in this area. You need to know which relationships are lethal and from such you should turn away. By putting God first, you'll also discover

which relationships are vital and necessary for your well-being.

Again, put God first and make Him your priority. As stated, you mean more to Him than the flowers of the field and the fowl of the air. So trust Him to provide as He facilitates your entire existence.

The following poems celebrate the fact that God will provide!

Matthew Six

Tomorrow is not promised
So we must be grateful
For today.

God's daily provisions
And continuous bread
He will never leave us
But love us instead.

Don't worry about tomorrow
Or fret about yester year
Don't let anxiety
Lead you into fear.

He clothed the grass of the field
Which today is and tomorrow is gone
The lilies are carefully arrayed
And the birds sing a lovely song.

Take no thought for tomorrow
Or what you will put on
Don't worry about food
To do so is wrong.

God satisfies
And meets our every need
We're destined to prosper
As one of Abraham's seed.

Always seek first
The kingdom of God
All else will be added
And your problems He'll resolve.

I will not complain
Neither be discontent
A day with the Lord
Is one very well spent.

My God made a vow
To always provide
Under His wings
I'll forever abide.

Tomorrow is not promised
We must focus on today
I will always trust You
Your Word, Lord, I'll obey.

Lord, Help Me!

Help me to accept
What You have for me.
Help me not to fight
Nor wrestle with Thee.

Help me to be grateful
And not discontent.
Help me to show mercy
And love that's heaven sent.

Help me to have faith
When my road seems hard
Help me to believe
Knowing that You're not far.

I have food, shelter, and clothing
Also the gift of time.
I'll focus on my plenty
And all that is mine.

My health is renewed
And my mind is at peace.
For this I sing praises
And my daily increase.

Lord, enlarge my coasts
And bless me indeed.
Keep Your hand upon me
Cause evil to flee.

Also help me
To never complain.
Only to be thankful
For what I have gained.

I'll proclaim Your goodness
Everywhere I go
I'll declare Your mercy
To those who don't know.

You as the Savior
And everlasting King
You as sovereign Ruler
Creator of everything.

Help me to fulfill
Your purpose for me
No more a senseless servant
But God's royalty.

Patience

"After he [Abraham] had patiently endured, he obtained the promise."
Hebrews 6:15

Lord, I want it now
Do I have to wait?
Patience is painful
Help me not to faint.

As slow as a river
The result and test of time
As endless as the sky
But in it you will find:

Hope for today
And a brighter tomorrow
Joy is coming
In exchange for your sorrow.

Patience will
Automatically come
It took a trial for you
Pain and suffering for some.

It's freely given
And has its reward
Read about Job
In God's Holy Word.

He had a unique dilemma
And all kinds of trouble
But because of patience
He received the double.

To my surprise
Some still didn't learn
From Job's example
So they continue to moan.

So often we rush
Through our waiting season
Relying on logic
And human reason.

Stay on the Potter's wheel
Until you are done
You will survive
And battles will be won.

Don't give up so easily
You will be made whole
Patience is a virtue
For your spirit, body, and soul.

Patience is also
A quality of love
Shown unto us
From God up above.

I know you don't like it
But please learn to wait
Have faith in the Master
He is never late!

Don't be anxious
Or go ahead of time
Please be patient
And wisdom you will find.

I choose rather to wait
And go through the process
Like Joshua I'll prosper
And have good success.

God won't give you
More than you can bear
He knows when to say,
"My child, you are there.

You have arrived
To inhabit Canaan land
You have endured
Now give yourself a hand.

Just like Abraham
You have passed the test.
Now you can enjoy
Your season of rest."

Lost and Found

"For the Son of Man is come to save that which was lost."
Matthew 18:11

Once I was lost
And couldn't find my way
I needed a hand
To guide me each day.

I looked to the east
And even went west
I traveled so far
My soul needed rest.

All I had to do
Was look up above
Your Spirit descended
Upon me like a dove.

You weren't lost
But I was in need
Your love captured me
Now I'm Yours indeed.

God, You're the One
And Lover of my soul
What a delight
To finally be made whole.

I love You with all
My heart and mind
Value and worth
In You I can find.

No mountain high
Can keep us apart
I'm Your friend forever
Right now from the start.

I have purpose and a mission
All wrapped up in one
I was called and chosen
Before my life begun.

No longer displaced
Or in a disarray
Desiring to live
And conquer each day.

Encourage yourself
Like I did indeed
The place called lost
Will never find me.

IV.

Issues

Of

Life

Decisions, Decisions, Decisions

One of the biggest issues of life is the art of making decisions. I call it an art because it takes skill to weigh all the consequences and arrive at the best choice in a timely manner. Some people are excellent decision makers. They consult wise counsel and are careful not to repeat mistakes of the past. Others are expert deliberators. They vacillate back and forth so much so that they have difficulty making up their own minds. And when they do, the opportunity for advancement has passed them by. Others because of impatience and lack of wisdom are abrupt in their decision making. They don't even think about the consequences. Instead, they jump into a commitment head first causing much dismay. Finally, there are those who are bound by fear. They fail to make any major decisions for fear of making the wrong one. They pass the baton to someone else and foolishly follow their lead.

When it comes to serving the Lord, some people are extremely indecisive. They're not sure if they want to commit to Him fully or serve Him on their own terms. These are those who have a God moment on Christmas and Easter, but forsake Him for the rest of the year. However, there is a population of believers who have decided to acknowledge the Lord in all their ways and live for Him throughout their days (Proverbs 3:5 and 6).

Israel has an interesting history. They, too, were indecisive when it came to serving the Lord. Their allegiance to Him was as consistent as a frozen lake in the summer time. In other words, they were quite unstable in their commitment. As long as God was parting the Red Sea, releasing water from a rock, or sending manna from heaven, their allegiance to Him was a given. But as soon as they thought Moses was on Mt. Sinai a little too long or that God had forsaken them, they were ready to return to Egypt. One can clearly conclude that their devotion was based on what God could do and not on Who He is. I don't care how many miracles He performed before their eyes, they continued to bombard Moses with murmurs and complaints and were never satisfied (Exodus 16).

Joshua, who proceeded Moses, was quite familiar with Israel's rebellious nature. This is why he presented them with the responsibility of making a choice. He already knew who he was going to serve. He just wanted God's Chosen to openly declare their loyalty and vow not to forsake the Lord once they entered Canaan. They had to decide. Would they serve the false gods of the Amorites or the true and living God of Abraham, Isaac, and Jacob? Joshua put it simply,

"...Choose you this day whom ye will serve..."

Joshua 24:15a

You, too, may be battling with the same dilemma. Will you reject the divine for the demonic and the sacred for the sensual? Or will you make a conscious effort to please the Lord? You make the choice and hopefully you will conclude like Joshua,

"...As for me and my house, we will serve the Lord."

Joshua 24:15c

In addition to choices, the following poems discuss some other issues pertinent to life. Included are such topics as love, family, and even forgiveness.

Choices

*"Choose you this day whom you will serve…but as for me and my house,
we will serve the Lord." Joshua 24:15*

Should I go to the left
Or should I go to the right
Should I serve the Lord
With all my might.

Should I love Him
And treat Him well
Should I bless Him
So I can tell.

Tell of His love
And prayers He'll hear
Tell of His grace
And the burdens He'll bear.

The choice is not hard
Just make sure you know
The Savior personally
Don't be His foe.

A bad decision
Made Adam and Eve
"Don't eat the fruit!"*
But they didn't take heed.

The Garden of Trees
Was once their home
Looking for covering
In shame they roamed.

Because of Adam's sin
We fell under the curse
But God promised a Savior
In Genesis 3, 15th verse.

In Abraham
We can rejoice
He left idol gods
That had no voice.

Joshua's loyalty
Makes him stand tall
An honorable leader
Destroyed Jericho's Wall.

Rahab the harlot
Chose the Hebrew God
And so did Moses
With faith and a rod.

The Hebrew boys
A stand they did take
Along with Daniel
They didn't forsake.

The Law of God
And His commandments
Before it was over
The king couldn't stand it.

How God showed up
In the den and fire
The devil again
Was proven a liar.

Mary and Martha
To name a few
Worshipped the Savior
What about you?

Paul and Silas
Prayed and did sing
From Peter and others
Praises did ring.

Who will you serve?
Is the question that be
I offer the Ruler
Of both land and sea.

Choices, choices
Consider these words
As for me and my house
We'll serve the Lord!

*Genesis 2:17

Life is so Unpredictable

Here today
Gone tomorrow
An even spread
Of joy and sorrow.

Sometimes we laugh
Sometimes we cry
Emotions fluctuate
Beyond the sky.

What we plan
Sometimes comes true
Then pain and fear
Will test me and you.

I don't have all the answers
But the Source I know
For strength and courage
To Him we can go.

As I travel
Throughout each day
His Spirit guides me
And shows me the way.

Unpredictable sometimes
Life can be
Yet in God
I rest peacefully.

Family

I was blessed to have
A two-parent home
Dad and Mom at the helm
And God on the throne.

I was blessed to have
A large family
We enjoyed much laughter
And even some grief.

I was blessed to be raised
In the church until grown
What a wonderful seed
My parents have sown.

We were always taught
To put God first
It brought us salvation
Escaping Satan's curse.

Children obey
Your parents in the Lord
That your days may be long
Upon God's green earth.

Fathers don't provoke
Your children to wrath
Mothers assist him
This is a great task.

Single parents everywhere
You're a fine, precious jewel
Use the Word as your weapon
Your sword and your tool.

We celebrate your strength
And your gift to maintain
A home full of order
Just let Jesus reign.

Train up your children
So they won't depart
Teach them to hide
The Word in their hearts.

Don't let the devil
Cause confusion
For the family is
A divine institution.

This is how
Your home should be
Representing God's love
With faith as the key.

We must preserve it
And strengthen family ties
A godly home
Is where love abides.

Death

"And as it is appointed unto man once to die, but after this the judgment."   *Hebrews 9:27*

I'll never understand
And I know this goes for you
How someone who is here
Is suddenly out of view.

Here today, gone tomorrow
Is seemingly what takes place
It happens so quickly
As part of the human race.

Rejoice when they go out
And weep when they come in
The Bible makes it clear
Speaking also against sin.

Yet it's hard to accept
When loved ones are gone
Death has been scheduled
Before we were born.

I don't clearly understand
But I accept it as truth
He is the sovereign God
In my old age and my youth.

Death, you have no victory
Because I will live again
There's a place for me
And a mansion in the plan.

Let's not view death
With negativity
It is your path
To eternity.

Just live your life
And value each day
God's love will guide
And show you the way.

I Will Focus on the Good

Although I have questions
I have come to one conclusion
Life is worth living
So I will focus on the good.

I sit here pondering
Over a full glass of hope
A plate full of faith
And several possibilities.

I choose to make a move
And not sit here frozen
Like an unaware deer
On life's busy highway.

I have good health
And I can breathe
My family is well
And I enjoy life's simple pleasures.

I choose to laugh
And experience peace
My motives are pure
And God is watching over me.

I will focus on the good
Because each day I move closer
To what God has for me
Never falling short
Of my destiny.

I will focus on the good.

Forgive and Forget

Forgive and forget
Let go of the past
Be thankful for today
And tomorrow's task.

Forgive and forget
Right now and here
Love self and others
Hold life so dear.

Forgive and forget
Is easy for you to say
But now I realize
It's the only way.

The way to truth
And a guiding light
The road to peace
And a longer life.

I'll never let
You control me
From guilt and shame
I am now free.

Release your offenders
And those who did you wrong
Refuse to hold a grudge
Put anger where it belongs.

Under your feet
Away from your heart
Let love abide
And do its part.

Forgive and forget
Let go of the past
Be thankful for today
And tomorrow's task.

V.

The

Female

Gender

"Did God save the best for last?"

A preacher once said that if God made anything better than a woman, He must have kept it for Himself. He concluded that Eve was God's finest work and the grand finale of His six-day creation. After this, God's work was complete and He designated the 7th day as one of rest.

Eve reflected the emotional side of Adam as well as the beauty and grace of God. She was the product of love and God's desire to give Adam a suitable mate. The animals had each other, but Adam needed someone to whom he could cleave. Eve satisfied this need and God affirmed it by making them one.

The woman was given all the vital parts needed to fulfill her several roles. As wife, mother, daughter, or friend, she is equipped to fall short in no area. She produces everywhere she goes and her value far exceeds anything on earth.

Join me as I celebrate the female gender and God's ability to make this human masterpiece.

A Woman's Story

Emotional, yes
Unreasonable, no
This is just the way we are.

Confident, yes
Conceited, no
This is just the way we are.

We can bear pain
And even laugh
We belong
To a special class.

We can build
And even give birth
Don't underestimate
What we're worth.

Sister Eve
Was the first
To be formed
Upon God's earth.

Handling so many
Things at one time,
As mother or a career
Nothing falls behind.

We can juggle
So many acts
Diversity
Is a fact.

By our man
Is where we stand
For support
And a helping hand.

Also making it
On our own
In wisdom and grace
We have grown.

Political genius
We can be
We were made
Phenomenally!

I'm trying to tell you
How it feels
To be empowered
With inner zeal.

We come in all
Shapes and sizes,
Sometimes predictable
Yet full of surprises.

From Adam's rib
We were made,
A woman's glory
Will never fade.

From a woman
The Savior was born,
With value and honor
Was Mary adorned.

The female gender
Is beyond compare
What's placed in our hands
Receives optimum care.

When we enter a room
All heads turn,
With grace we ascend
With patience we learn.

How to endure
And even survive
Complete was Adam
When Eve arrived.

We've learned to master
Whatever comes our way
When God made woman
It was a wonderful day!

The Devotion of a Woman

The devotion of a woman
Is hard to perceive
Her husband counts it a privilege
In his heart she's well received.

Her integrity is pure
And her wisdom runs deep
When two become one
In love it should keep.

The devotion of a woman
Is seen in her home
Where she occupies
Her female throne.

The single woman portrays
A special gift of her own
Determined to make it
From the day she was born.

A mother will always
Take care of her seed
Not selfish or haughty
Just meeting a need.

What would Adam have done
Had he remained alone?
He would have questioned God
Cried, ached, and moaned.

Adam was grateful
When God made woman
From her proceeds life
She produces every moment.

The devotion of a woman
Valued beyond silver and gold
Having beauty and flare
Yet a mystery to unfold.

The New Feminist

We aim high
And never look low
Enjoying our journey
And where we must go.

Our plight is simple
Yet complex as it seems
Emerging from the earth
Like a Phoenix and blazing beam.

A thunderous storm
When necessary
Then a gentle dove
In life's sanctuary.

We have a cause against
Gender inequality
We love you, men
But degradation will never be.

We can be your friend
Wanting not to be your foe
We'd rather be your partner
So in peace we can grow.

We live each day
With a vibrant thrust
We respect you for
Being made first.

We were made from your rib
To walk by your side
We're willing to submit
Letting you be the guide.

Yet making it clear
For all to see
Declaring a word
Of equality.

Our beauty is from within
Reigning from without
We have arrived
Having very few doubts.

Many of us
Have made history
As we tell
Our own story.

I love being a woman
So I can flaunt my grace
The verdict is in
So I rest my case!

VI.

The

Male

Seed

The Value of Dust

God knew the value of dust before the world began. This is why He chose it rather than dirt to make man, the crowning glory of His creative work (Psalm 8:5). In addition to this, God gave Adam the authority to name all the animals (Genesis 2:19, 20). He trusted Adam and knew that he would use his authority correctly. Therefore, He gave him the power to reign and subdue all that was placed upon the earth.

Even though Adam made a wrong choice, there was an immediate display of God's grace. Influenced by the serpent, Adam ate the forbidden fruit. Yet God declared that Satan would be destroyed and man restored to his rightful place (Genesis 3:15).

On this note, we celebrate the male seed and the fact that he was made in the image of God. Given a place of prominence, He is to execute his authority with strength, stamina, and integrity. As the head, man serves as a covering and his esteemed position should never be taken lightly. Therefore,

Fathers, we laud you
For the priestly role
You have established
In your home.

Son, we honor you
For continuing the legacy
Of those
Who have gone.

Brother, we praise you
For paving the way
For those who are
To come.

And Lord, we thank You
For making man
To glorify
The Son.

Together let's celebrate the male seed, the crowning glory of
all creation.

In His Image

What a wonderful thing
Our heavenly Father did
Making man in
His own image.

What a wonderful thought
To occupy God's mind
Then came into being
Flesh and spirit intertwined.

God wouldn't let
The opportunity pass
To present Adam
As a completed task.

He was given dominion
And told to rule the earth
We are Adam's descendents
Continuing to give birth.

Only man could give God
What He wanted from the beginning
Someone to reflect His love
With worship ascending.

Then God said, "I'll rest."
After working for six days
The seventh belongs to Him
Rejoice and give Him praise.

In God's likeness man was made
To bring Him glory and honor
The serpent didn't succeed
He was cursed and left to ponder.

Adam's disobedience
Brought a sinful circumstance
Then along came Jesus
Giving man a second chance.

Satan will never
Dwell in God's heaven
Only man has the right
To live in His presence.

Be sure to reflect
The image of love
As given to us
From God up above.

Be sure to reflect
Creativity
Using the gifts and talents
That were given to thee.

Be sure to reign
In power and dominion
Rebuking the devil
Destroying Satan's kingdom.

Honor your Maker
And Creator of us all
In dignity you live
And forever stand tall.

Adam, Adam

You were made
To subdue the earth
With God given authority
You're the ruler of us all.

When God made the animals
The birds, flowers, and trees
He said it was good
Leaving something still undone.

There was no one for worship
No one for fellowship
And there was no one
To till the ground.

So God took the dust
Not dirt, but the fine part
And made man
In His image and in His likeness.

God breathed into man's nostrils
His own breath of life
Man became a living soul
To fulfill a highly esteemed position.

God gave man intelligence
Because His Spirit was in him
He named the animals
But still he was alone.

Adam needed someone fit
And designed just for him
Then along came Eve
To answer the call.

God placed them in the garden
The Garden of Eden it was called
Everything that they needed
Was at their disposal.

He gave them food
There was air and even water
"But don't touch that tree!"
Is all that God commanded.

Man made a wrong move
The serpent beguiled Eve
Eve convinced Adam
And we were all brought under condemnation.

Then came Jesus
And we were given
Another chance
At hope and life eternal.

The plan of salvation
Has lifted the curse
And the deeds of Satan
Are completely nullified.

You may have fallen
But in God you can get up
To regain your authority
And place of preeminence.

We need you to reign
To keep things in order
Like God intended
Before the world began.

In the eyes of God
You are royalty
And your dominion was approved
From on high.

Adam, Adam
Take your rightful place
With God as your guide
Showing you the way.

In Unity

Man and woman
Side by side
Not divided
To collide.

From the rib
God did make
For Mr. Adam
A suitable mate.

She was fit
To be his friend
A wife and lover
God did send.

Eve was given
A major part
A starring role
Right from the start.

Father of all
Mother of earth
This wonderful union
Was God's first.

Man must leave
His father and mother
They must cleave
To each other.

Two as one
Is a mystery
It can be done
In unity.

A glorious couple
Together we make
Man and woman
For kingdom's sake!

VII.

Something

To

Think

About

Time to Reconsider
Commentary on Genesis 22

One benefit of reading the Bible is that I always walk away with something to think about. I'm equally inspired by God's relationship with man and the miracles that He performed on behalf of His people.

Genesis 22 has special meaning to me because it has been my focus of study for almost five years. Each time I read it, I gain further insight and a renewed appreciation for the testing ability of God. He knows how much we can endure and what it takes for us to qualify for the next dimension. So when He told Abraham to sacrifice his son, He did so knowing that he would pass the test. God knew that he would be the example of faith for generations to come. This is why He chose Abraham, entrusted him with great wealth, and equipped him to become the father of many nations. Allow me to visit this chapter hopefully giving you something to think about. And always remember that when you have time to reconsider, it's really time to exercise faith.

In Genesis 22, God shares with us one of the most profound Bible stories written. It is here that He tests Abraham by asking him to sacrifice his long awaited son, Isaac. This incident portrays the importance of giving God what you value the most, trusting Him when He tells you to do something that seemingly contradicts His character, and the reality of John 3:16 which says,

"For God so loved the world, that He gave his only begotten Son, that whosoever believeth in him should not perish, but have everlasting life."

After reading Genesis 22 for the millionth time, several revelations jumped from the pages. One of which is the fact that Abraham and Isaac had more than enough time to reconsider and go another way opposite of what God commanded. God gave them very little details about their quest and journey to the mountain. Yet they both moved in obedience and faith achieving a victorious end.

It took Abraham and Isaac several days to get to the mountain that they knew not of. In other words, Abraham didn't know the exact location where he was to sacrifice his son. Without having any specific instructions, he moved in faith trusting that God would fill in the details as Isaac and he went along. Yes, this journey took several days, which, again, gave them ample time to reconsider and go another way.

On the third day (verse 4), Abraham lifted up his eyes and saw the place (the mountain) afar off. He had several more days ahead of him before he actually reached the exact location. He could have easily said, "Lord, this is a bit much. I don't know where I'm going, these mountains are extremely far, and You want me to sacrifice my son. I think I'll go another way to a place I know of: home." During this time span, between points A and B, Abraham could have let his own will, feedback from the devil, and plain old common sense influence his decision to obey God. Yet he continued to walk the walk of faith with apparent uncertainties to a high place. Here he would sacrifice his only beloved son like God did His only begotten Son on the cross of Golgotha's Hill. Isaac was a type of Christ because Jesus and he laid down their lives in obedience to their Father.

Not only did Abraham have time to reconsider, Isaac did also. They were in the midst of several mountains and because of Isaac's youth, he could have easily taken off running...especially when he came to the realization that, "Father, I see the fire and the wood. But where is the sacrifice? Where is the lamb that is to be offered (verse 7)?" In my opinion, this would have been the most opportune time for Isaac's great escape. Yet he stayed in obedience to his father.

He could have taken off perhaps getting lost amongst all those mountains. Even after Abraham took him and tied him to the altar, Isaac, because of his youth, could have broken himself loose from this entire set-up and Abraham would have never caught him. Can you imagine a man in his hundreds chasing a lad of about 14 or 15 years old amongst all those mountains? What a sight! This was the perfect time for Isaac's getaway. Yes, we always commend Abraham for his faith, but much can be said about Isaac. He, too, deserves some accolades. We must applaud him for trusting his father enough to go along with the plan. He had less information than Abraham about this journey to the mountain, but he trusted his father that God would provide a sacrifice and that his dad and he would return. According to Abraham, they were just going up to worship (verse 5). I also believe that Abraham and Isaac knew enough about God to question the very thing that God was asking them to do. God required the blood of goats and bulls. And even though Leviticus 18:21 had not yet been written, I'm sure the whole concept of sacrificing his son raised some red flags. But they both were obedient and moved in faith!

Leviticus 18:21 reads,

"Thou shalt not let any of thy seed pass through the fire of Molech."

The heathen nations sacrificed their children to the false god, Molech. But God made it clear to the children of Israel that they were not to participate in such heathenish practices. Sacrificing your children, according to Leviticus 18:21, was clearly an abomination! How mind-boggling. Like I said, even though Leviticus 18:21 had not yet been written, I'm sure Abraham knew enough about God to say, "Hmmm, this is a bit strange. God is telling me to sacrifice my son. Yet, I will obey."

What do you do when God seemingly contradicts Himself? You move in obedience. This is why it is so important to know His voice. He'll tell you what to do and when to do it. Therefore, you must move in obedience even when there are some apparent uncertainties. Become acquainted with God's still small voice, go as far as He tells you to go and stop when He says stop, even if it is in midair.

Abraham undoubtedly knew the voice of God. With little to no details, he did what the Lord said even though his son and he had time to reconsider. Remember, the journey to the mountain wasn't a straight shot and it took several days to get there. To top it off, God was seemingly contradicting Himself by telling Abraham to do something that was later forbidden in Leviticus 18:21. Abraham obeyed the Lord and Isaac obeyed his father even though they both were put in an extremely precarious predicament.

Lord help us to do what You say even when we don't understand, have very few details and there's time to reconsider. Help us to know Your voice because if Abraham didn't he would have forfeited this entire experience. He probably would have never gone up the mountain in the first place. Worst than this, he wouldn't have recognized the voice of the angel when he told Abraham to stop and do Isaac no harm. While Abraham's hand and knife were in midair about to come down and slay Isaac, the angel of the Lord intercepted and shouted from heaven,

"Lay not thine hand upon the lad, neither do thou anything unto him: for now I know that thou fearest God, seeing thou hast not withheld thy son, thine only son from me. And Abraham lifted up his eyes, and looked, and behold behind him a ram caught in a thicket by his horns: and

Abraham went and took the ram, and offered him up for a burnt offering in the stead of his son." Verses 12 and 13

Like many of us, Abraham could have easily mistaken the voice of the angel for that of the devil. He could have been adamant about doing what God told him to do. He would have wrongfully rebuked the devil rather than taking heed to these last minute instructions and sudden change of plans. It can happen so quickly. We can be on our way doing what the Lord said do and He immediately says, "STOP! Don't go any further. I was just testing your faith." We have to be that sensitive and in tune with Him so that we won't miss any last minute instructions. Last minute instructions are vital. Therefore, we must be open to the sudden move of God, become familiar with His voice, and follow directions up until the very end.

In conclusion, Abraham and Isaac had time to reconsider. First, they did not know the exact mountain and location where the sacrifice was to take place. In addition, the journey took several days and the instructions were seemingly contradictory. Finally, Isaac could have taken off running and Abraham would have never caught him because of the mountainous region and his old age. What do you do between points A and B? What do you do when there is time to reconsider and you have the opportunity to go another way? What do you do if you are ever put in a similar situation or given questionable instructions? I suggest the following:

- First and foremost you must trust God!
- Second, know the voice of God.
- Third, keep a praise in your mouth and worship in your heart.
- Fourth, stay focused on what God told you to do, but be open for last minute instructions.
- Next, think, talk and walk faith.

- Also, don't be like Jonah who tried to get away and ended up in the belly of a great fish.
- Lastly, be careful how much you share with others. If Abraham had shared with his friends what God told him to do, undoubtedly, they would have written him off as mad. Then they would have tried with all their power to talk him out of it. Instead, Abraham's words were few. He simply said that his son and he were going to worship and that they would be back (verse 5).

When you have time to reconsider and God's instructions seemingly contradict His own nature, walk by faith and not by sight. Your five senses won't be able to comprehend what your faith and obedience will. And your human logic is always minuscule in comparison to spiritual discernment. So rely on what you already know about God and decide from the onset to do things His way. You'll obtain favor with Him and man and a testimony that will last for generations. Favor and a testimony are valuable assets that should be coveted more than riches and gold. Don't forfeit your experiences with God by trying to figure Him out. Instead of requiring so many details, walk with Him and learn from Him. And when there's time to reconsider, use it as an opportunity to exercise faith! The following poems are simply something to think about. Bask in the presence of God's Word and let Him speak to your heart.

Testimony

Abraham's Testimony:
"I didn't know God
I worshipped idols
Because of my faith
Father of Nations is my title."

Joseph's Testimony:
"From prison to the palace
From a pit I did moan
As a God-ordained leader
I ruled from Pharaoh's throne."

Hannah's Testimony:
"All I wanted
Was a male child
Then Samuel was born
After a long while."

Job's Testimony:
"I lost everything
Not knowing what to say
I decided not to curse God
Choosing rather to pray."

The Hebrew boys' Testimony:
"In the fiery furnace
Flames we did see
Then Jesus appeared
Now four men, not three."

The woman with the issue of blood
Wasn't even given a name
Because of her faith
She won worldly acclaim.

Mary Magdalene
Once possessed with the devil
Chose to worship God
And not be a rebel.

We all have a story to tell
How we were broken and even rejected
Then subdued by God's love
And in His arms we're protected.

Don't keep it to yourself
All that God has done
Proclaim His goodness
And worship His Son.

Allow me to tell
How He gave me wealth
Spiritual joy
And even divine health.

So look up my sister
Hey brother, raise your voice
Use your mouth to praise Him
And your hands to rejoice!

Go tell the world
All that God did
Because your testimony
Should never be hid.

The Comforter Has Come

"And I will pray the Father, and He shall give you another Comforter that He may abide with you forever." John 14:16

He who was left
To continue the mission
He says what God says
And glorifies the Son.

He is our empowerment
Making us a witness
As far as Judea
And Jerusalem, too.

He will settle
Your broken heart
He brings you peace
In the midst of your storm.

The revealer of truth
My inspiration and revelation
Giver of joy
And a right relationship with God.

He imparts the gifts
And fruit of the Spirit
To edify the body and build us up
Through Him, we can lay hands.

Cast out devils
Heal the sick
Dunamis He's often called
Making me a militant soldier.

He's everywhere
At the same time
Imparting wisdom and knowledge
Discernment and understanding.

"I will not leave you comfortless,"
Is what Jesus said
The Holy Ghost lives within
Working the wonders of the Lord.

He will abide with you forever
The Comforter
Which is the Holy Ghost
Which the Father has sent in Jesus' Name.

He will teach you and remind you
Lead you and guide you
Caress you and arrest you
Hold you and mold you.

He proceeds from the Father
Testifying of the Son
Jesus had to depart
So the Comforter could come.

Like Jesus
He ministers to the world
The Father, the Son, and the Holy Ghost
Are equal partners in my redemption!

For Such a Time as This

You were called like Queen Esther
To save someone from disaster
Use your talents and your gifts
To give someone a soulish lift.

Your purpose you must fulfill
You can't leave earth until
You have reached your destiny
And what you were born to be.

God's mighty love and tender care
Will take you on your journey there
Satan's schemes will never win
His time is short and running thin.

His former power he won't regain
He fell from grace, but Jesus reigns
On this day you've been called
So catch someone before he falls.

Tell someone about God's love
Shown and given from above
Tell someone about salvation
That's available to every nation.

Tell about how He lives
The peace and joy that He gives
Tell about His amazing grace
And how to run this Christian race.

You've been called to encourage
Along life's path and winding voyage
This is the time and the day
For you to show someone the way.

Don't deny God's mighty power
Take advantage of this hour
Don't diminish your ability
And your call to destiny.

You were called like Queen Esther
To save someone from disaster
For such a time as today
Please show someone the way.

What If?

What if God
Had left me in
The terrible state
I was in?

What if He
Had turned His head
Withdrew His grace
Judgment instead?

What if God
Sent not His Son
To save the world
And souls be won?

What if sickness
And death had power
Victory would
Not be ours?

What if I
Failed to see
That I have
Dignity?

Or even failed
To realize
I'm God's trophy
And His prize?

I'm glad I don't
Have to ponder
All these thoughts
And senseless wonder.

One thing I
Am sure of
Is God's mercy
And His love.

Instead of sickness
I am healed
No more voids
But I'm filled.

I have conquered
Even death
The recipient of
Heaven's best.

The beauty of
His wonderful Son
Abides within
And makes us one.

With His Word
My path He lights
I have soared
To new heights.

I have favor
On my side
To God my thoughts
I can confide.

And to Him
I can go
He'll say yes, wait
Or no.

I'm glad He didn't
Leave me in
The awful state
I was in.

He chose to keep
And renew my mind
Oh what peace
And joy divine.

Doors of Opportunities

"I know thy works: behold, I have set before thee an open door, and no man can shut it." Revelation 3:8

Open doors of opportunities
Are right before your face
Take advantage of this time
Walk at a steady pace.

Please do not take too long
Or else it'll pass you by
And maybe never come again
So grab it while it's nigh.

The earth contains everything
That you'll ever need
So look to those who have gone
Before you and take heed.

There's no telling just how far
In life you will soar
With a positive attitude
You'll accomplish so much more.

I wish you well and God's speed
As you take your rightful place
Amongst the heroes of our time
Who refused to play it safe.

Don't be afraid to walk on water
Jesus will take your hand
Look to Him in faith believe
And you'll possess the land.

Excuses should from your mouth
Never, ever proceed
Positive confessions are the way
That you will succeed.

Open doors of opportunities
Are right before your face
God is right by your side
To help you win the race.

Now it's time to enjoy
All that you've worked for
So settle down and take your rest
He'll give you so much more.

VIII.

A

Day

To

Remember

The Most Memorable Day

9/11/01 has come to be one of the most memorable days in American history. On this day we suffered one of the deadliest attacks within our borders. In a matter of minutes our lives were changed never to be the same again. New York City, Washington, DC, and Pennsylvania were stunned beyond belief and homeland security is now a concern of us all.

As a result of this day, many have learned to value even the simplest things in life. Peace and safety are now commodities. And when one goes to work and returns home unharmed, for this we are truly grateful.

The happenings on 9/11 are still fresh in my mind. I remember how I sat frozen and glued to the TV in utter dismay. I couldn't believe that the same people who we trusted to reside in our country became our worst enemies. The strength of the Twin Towers dwindled to dust and the hole in the ground was also evident in our hearts.

In the midst of anger and innumerable questions, 9/11 was the day that I started writing. I had no idea that six years latter my writings would develop into a book. Fortunately, my pen and paper helped me to sift through my thoughts as I tried to make sense of it all.

Please allow me to share my heart as I reflect on what I still consider the most memorable day.

Mixed Feelings

(Author's Note: My reaction to the WTC attack on 9/11/01)

I'm not sure
How I feel
At first I really
Wanted to kill.

Or send them back
From where they came
Arabs return
To your own homeland.

God said pray
To correct this wrong
But I didn't want
To sing this song.

I wanted them
To feel the pain
That they caused
And were to blame.

Yet they're all
Not like that
Not all support
Terrorist attacks.

Some just want
To live in peace
They, too, desire
For wars to cease.

This may be true
So we need a plan
To rid civilization
Of this evil man.

Bin Laden formed
What came to be
America's worst
Catastrophe.

He carefully planned
And orchestrated
What his men
Executed.

O, how wicked
One man can be
To shake our sense
Of sanity.

Yet we found
Strength in each other
And were moved to love
One another.

Again God said
That we must pray
I chose this time
That I'd obey.

He made everything
Both evil and good
For His will
Like He should.*

I pray that terrorism
Will come to an end
With God on our side
America will win.

*Proverbs 16:4

9/11

This is the day
We won't forget
A day of great terror
Not ever met.

They felt this was
The only way
To express their feelings
They caused dismay.

Some Arabs disagree
With our government
To befriend Israel
Causes them contempt.

But God said pray
For His chosen ones
Then blessings will flow
Beyond the sun.

America must turn
Back to God
And serve the Lord
'Til we die.

Then we'll better
Understand
God's perfect will
And His plan.

I must rehearse
What took place
As buildings fell
Before my face.

They hijacked four
Planes with knives
Taking many
Innocent lives.

Planes went crashing
Into the World Trade Center
Buildings tumbled
Being nothing thereafter.

Smoke filled the sky
With fire and debris
Bodies in midair
From windows some did flee.

A third plane we saw
Destroyed part of the Pentagon
Washington was hit
Innocent lives were gone.

Headed for the White House
Was thought the fourth plane
It crashed in Pennsylvania
Their mission was maimed.

Many lives were lost
The passengers and crew
I hope the terrorists
Will get what their due.

The towers were destroyed
And buildings nearby
The heat from the jets
Brought terror from on high.

Corpses were recovered
Limbs and body parts
Some even escaped
And were able to depart.

The United States
Soon went to war
We really need to pray
And seek God to the core.

O, God, we need
Direction from You
If we don't get it
What will we do?

Perhaps you will bless us
Like you did Jehosophat
All he did was praise You
And You launched the attack.

Psalms 46 says,
"You cause wars to cease."
Maybe this will be
Our answer to peace.

Look upon our president
And other leaders, too
America please pray
Everyone and not a few.

Terrorists you must know
That God's love is sure
Don't let evil trap you
Into Satan's lure.

He will only fool you
And lead you to destruction
His game is never fair
But leads to corruption.

God only wants
For us to seek His face
So we'll be blessed
And take our rightful place.

Then we will hear
From God Who's in heaven
So something like this
Will again never happen.

Scripture to consider:

"I exhort therefore, that, first of all, supplications, prayers, intercessions, and giving of thanks, be made for all men: For kings, and for all that are in authority; that we may lead a quiet and peaceable life in all godliness and honesty. For this is good and acceptable in the sight of God our Savior. Who will have all men to be saved, and to come unto the knowledge of the truth." I Timothy 2:1- 4

IX.

TRIBUTES

"Render therefore to all their dues: tribute to whom tribute is due; custom to whom custom; fear to whom fear; honour to whom honour."

Romans 13:7

Always Remember

This section called, *Tributes*, is dedicated to those who have secured a special place in my heart. Some have gone to be with the Lord, while others are yet among us. The Bible tells us to give honor to whom honor is due. Therefore, we can't forget those who are in authority, who have made a difference, and have impacted our lives in a very prominent way.

I took this opportunity to honor my father and sister. If you have ever lost someone dear to you, it's not at all difficult to keep their memory alive. God was gracious enough to lend them to my family. When their mission was complete, He took them home. Also included is a family tribute to my mother presented to her on her 70th birthday. If your mother is still alive be sure to honor her. Cherish her and constantly remind her that her sacrifices will never go unnoticed.

Lastly, there is a tribute to pastors. Even when they're overworked and overlooked, they continue to feed God's flock. God specifically commands us to pray for them and we are also to obey them. Pastors are worthy of double honor as they watch over our souls (I Timothy 5:17, 18; Hebrews 13:17). Therefore, we should be grateful for their courageous leadership and how they strategically guide us into the Promised Land.

Enjoy these tributes and maybe you can create some of your own. Never forget those who have paved the way making it easier for you to live a more successful life.

Honoring My Father

A tribute to my father, Elmo Spencer:
Sunrise: 1/28/33   Sunset: 6/17/05   Celebration: 6/23/05

I never knew a man
Who exhibited such power
His strength was evident
Even in his final hour.

God saw fit
To take Daddy home
But while on earth
He established his personal throne.

As head of household
He did rule well
We honored and loved him
Listening as he would tell:

His funny jokes
And playing catchy tunes
On his harmonica
Joy filling the room.

A fabulous dresser
And excellent cook
Providing for his family
Something he never forsook.

Counselor and historian
Talking about the old days
Keeping us together
United is what he prayed.

I never knew a man
Who was "sharp" all the time
Dunkin Donuts coffee
Would suit him just fine.

He was an early riser
Never sleeping past six
Whatever was broken
He was able to fix.

He didn't believe
In over spending
"Save your money!"
He was always hinting.

He was a fine example
To everyone, especially me
An ideal picture
Of what a man should be.

I desire a husband
Just like Dad
When you left
I was extremely sad.

Happy because
You're no longer in pain
What I lost
Was heaven's gain.

Sad because
I miss you everyday
But God knows best
Despite what I say.

I try not to question
His sovereign will
I had a void
That now He fills.

I long to see you, Daddy
On the porch you would sit
Greeting the neighbors
And sharing your wit.

He's resting now
Can't wait to see him
Daddy, you are
My hero and champion!

Although I miss you
God knew what was best
Sleep on Daddy
You have passed the test.

A devoted husband
And friend to all
The epitome of honor
You yet stand tall.

You taught us all
What it meant to be a man
You covered your family
The way God planned.

It's hard to say good-bye
But you're in a better place
Soon and very soon
I'll see you face to face.

Dear Sister

In honor of my sister, Jacqueline D. Spencer:
Sunrise: 12/19/60   Sunset: 2/7/01   Celebration: 2/12/01

Your beautiful voice
Would fill the air
Setting the tone
And the atmosphere.

You sang like an angel
As you gave God praise
Causing us to rejoice
And our hands we would raise.

I don't know why
God took you so young
Perhaps a song was needed
In heaven to be sung.

You have joined
God's heavenly choir
Still to remain
Our heart's desire.

You left a legacy
Through the son that you bore
Your lovely memory
Continues to soar.

You reached out to others
As a counselor and friend
Your impact on earth
Will never end.

A daughter and sister
Fantastic mother, too
There is no other
In comparison to you.

I think about you, Jackie
Each and everyday
Your laughter and smile
And the things you would say.

You stood tall
Wherever you went
I know for sure
You were heaven sent.

Long Live the Queen!

A Tribute to My Mother

A woman of grace
She is described
Epitome of strength
By Daddy's side.

Always generous
To those in need
Never destructive
Just planting a seed.

Surrounding me with love
Yet giving me space
A wide, beautiful smile
Still decorates her face.

Rearing five children
With different personalities
She mentored us all
Very carefully.

Strong disciplinarian
Full of wisdom all the time
Of all the mothers
I'm glad she is mine!

Wife, mother, friend
Fulfilling each role
Extending her heart
To every living soul.

Giving us standards
And values by which to live
A listening ear
She would always give.

Her grandchildren adore her
Nieces and nephews, too
Family and friends
Just to name a few.

This tribute is short
Compared to her worth
She always taught us
To put God first.

I present unto you
The world's greatest mother
Given to us
From our Heavenly Father.

Keshia and her mother, Joyce Jean Spencer, at her 70th birthday party, August 19, 2006, Westampton, NJ

To Pastors Everywhere

"And I will give you pastors according to mine heart, which shall feed you with knowledge and understanding." Jeremiah 3:15

This tribute is for you
Called to lead God's flock
This prayer is for you,
"Draw strength from the Rock!"

Sometimes it seems
That you're standing alone
Each day your cry
Goes before God's throne.

But know that God
And people in your care
Will never leave you
Yes, we'll be there.

Thank you for all
The sacrifices you make
Not for you
But for our sake.

Thank you for rightly
Dividing the Word
And teaching us how
To live in this world.

Your example of
Integrity and faith
Portraying to all
God's amazing grace.

Undying devotion
Is how you serve
When there is trouble
You seem unnerved.

You bless our children
Weddings and funerals, too
There is no end
To all that you do.

For your dedication
And commitment to the church
We acknowledge your greatness
And proclaim your worth.

Thank you for leading us
Into the Promised Land
With the spiritual armor
And sword in your hand.

God truly called you
To fulfill a special task
Whatever you need
He said, "Just ask."

You feed us all
With spiritual understanding
Upon your life
Is a special anointing.

Continue to lead us
With knowledge and wisdom
Teaching us the principles
Of living in God's kingdom.

We appreciate all
That you say and do
This tribute and prayer
Goes out to you.

X.

Short Stories

Don't Settle for Ishmael, Wait on Isaac

(the Blessing vs. the Promise)

"And as for Ishmael, I have heard thee: behold I have blessed him...But my covenant will I establish with Isaac, which Sarah shall bear unto thee at this set time in the next year." Genesis 17:20-21

The following account is a true story about a woman's decision to refuse Ishmael and wait on Isaac. To give it more credence, I'll tell it in the first person. Hopefully, it will encourage you not to settle for a blessing, but wait on the promise. Endure until you receive God's BEST, rather than settle for a MESS!

A few years ago, I was engaged to a man. To most, our engagement was inevitable because we had dated off and on for so long. Honestly, the engagement was unsettling because God told me on our very first date that he wasn't the one. But I wanted to get married so bad that I was willing to ignore the word of the Lord and do my own thing. This on and off relationship lasted for about ten years because every time we would break up, I would take him right back. Why? I'm not sure. Perhaps I enjoyed having someone in my life. And when someone is good to you (good, I might add, is a relative term), it's hard to give him up. We are creatures of habit and I think subconsciously I subscribed to the thought that, "The wrong man is better than no man at all." So we stayed together, attempted to get married, then God intervened.

Throughout this crazy relationship I was always honest. I told this fellow time and time again that God said he wasn't the one. He would then ask, "Does God mean now or never?" My response would simply be, "He said you're not the one." Yet I allowed him to remain in my life. We equally were in denial and tried to hold on to something we knew would never be. I always thought I had the upper hand because I had received a Word from the Lord. Also, I think I had a little more class. If someone would have told me, "God said you are not the one," I would have headed for the hills in defense of my own pride. BUT YET HE STAYED. On the other hand, if I had exercised better judgment, I would have ended this relationship, no questions asked. BUT YET I STAYED. This roller coaster ride continued and as a result I stayed and he stayed, but God never changed His mind. He wasn't the one and we had the nerve to get engaged. Let's see what the Word says in order to give my story more clarity.

Throughout this entire ordeal I became well acquainted with Father Abraham and Mother Sarah. God had me in Genesis, Romans, and Hebrews every time He needed to remind me of some things. He knew that this man was good to me and it was going to be hard for me to give him up. He also knew what I didn't know: The brother was being "good" to a whole lot of other women in addition to me. (How he did it I don't know because he was always in my face! But this is a whole 'nother story which I may not have time to get into.) Yes, he was good to me and God Himself agreed that this man was a blessing, but he wasn't the promise. God knew that he had qualities I couldn't resist. He was caring, generous, and very thoughtful, but still was not the promise. This is where most of us get mixed up. We settle for the blessing because it feels so good. But God wants us to wait on the promise because it will last forever. Your first apartment was a blessing because it was a sign of your independence, but your 5BR home is the promise because it represents ownership. Your Toyota was a blessing because it got you around, but your new Jaguar is the promise because it's a sign of prominence. Your Bozo was a blessing because he bought you a set of lamps, but Boaz is the promise because he is attached to your destiny. Again, this is where we mess up. We settle for the blessing because it is easily accessible and we miss the promise because it seems so far away. But I guarantee if you wait on God, you will obtain a good report and that which He spoke over your life before the world began. The promise will come to pass. We just have to respect God's plan, purpose, and pace. Now let's get back to Abraham and Sarah.

Abraham was the father of faith and a friend of God. Against all odds, he believed God and knew that Isaac would come. Even though it didn't happen right away, Abraham held on to the promise because he knew that it was impossible for God to lie. Though the vision tarries, wait for it. It will surely come. God spoke to Abraham in Genesis 15:4-6,

"...He that shall come forth out of thine own bowels shall be thine heir...And he [Abraham] believed in the Lord; and [H]e counted it to him for righteousness."

Then Sarah's carnal plan in Genesis 16 tried to abort the promise. Yet God reminded Abraham that Sarah in her old age would have a son and a substitute for Isaac would never be (Genesis 17:15-22). Sarah, like most of us, got real impatient and made a hasty decision. Because of this, we have two warring nations that continue to fight until this day (Jews [Isaac] and Arabs [Ishmael]). Be very careful!!! Your hasty decision can affect generations to come and a war that may never end.

Like God told me, He is simply saying to you: Don't settle and please don't try to help Him out. He knows exactly what He is doing so STOP! You're about to do something that you will regret for the rest of your life. What you do today can infect your tomorrow and change the course of your life. So don't do it!

Yes, my ex-fiancé was a blessing, but he wasn't the promise. Marrying him would have prevented me from reaching my personal Canaan in a timely manner. Canaan represents the purpose that God has for you which is a land flowing with milk and honey. He wants you to possess and occupy. But you must cooperate with Him so that you won't wander in the wilderness unnecessarily (Deut. 1:8, 25).

Isaac was the promise and Ishmael was the blessing, but they couldn't dwell together (Gen. 21:10). This would have caused a major conflict so there had to be a separation. Promise and Bondage can't live under the same roof because their intentions are drastically different. Therefore, one had to go, and it wasn't Isaac. In like manner, I was the child of promise and my fiancé was Ishmael. And one had to go. There had to be a separation. Even though I knew this and God had spoken to me plainly, I still persisted in what I wanted to do. So God had to reveal some things. Three months before the wedding, while I was addressing the wedding invitations, I realized that he was still involved with the ex-wife, ex-girlfriend, and God knows who else. We had our rings, gown, tuxedo, and the invitations were about to be mailed. Money was put down on the reception hall, my girls were fitted and the word was out that I was getting married. Yet it never came to pass. What God said He meant and He wasn't going to change His mind for anyone, not even me. My heart was broken and I thought that I would never love again. But when God says no, that is what He means, NO! So don't try to change His mind. It will never happen. He may allow some things, but ultimately His will is going to be done, either through you or someone else. God gives us choices because He created us as free moral agents. The truth of the matter is that we have to live with our choices. So I suggest that you follow His lead because He knows the end at the beginning.

Yes, I became very much acquainted with Abraham & Sarah as God guided me through this ordeal. I wanted so bad to settle because I was tired of being single. It seemed like everyone was getting married and I didn't want to be left out. In fact, two other couples were getting married around the same time. As purpose would have it, everyone made it down the isle, but me. At this point, I was devastated and really needed someone to comfort my soul. This is when God stepped in again.

He encouraged me by simply saying, "Better things". Yes, He had better things for me that accompany salvation and He didn't want me to miss it. Let's go to the scripture.
Hebrews 6:9-15 says,

"But beloved, we are persuaded better things of you, and things that accompany salvation, though we thus speak. For God is not unrighteous to forget your work and labour of love, which ye have shewed towards His name in that ye have ministered to the saints and do minister...And so, after he [Abraham] had patiently endured, he obtained the promise. "

Patience...Endurance...hmmmmm.

Then God took me to Romans 4:16-22,

"...He [Abraham] staggered not at the promise of God through unbelief; but was strong in faith, giving glory to God; and being fully persuaded that, what He had promised, He was able also to perform..."

I was then led to Hebrews 10:35-39,

"Cast not away therefore your confidence, which hath great recompense of reward. For ye have need of patience, that, after ye have done the will of God, ye might receive the promise. For yet a little while, and he that shall come will come, and will not tarry. Now the just shall live by faith: but if any man draw back, my soul shall have no pleasure in him.

But we are not of them who draw back unto perdition: but of them that believe to the saving of the soul."

God was speaking to me all along because He didn't want me to make the biggest mistake of my life. I was about to marry the wrong guy and miss what He had in store for me: promise. I was willing to settle for Ishmael and forsake Isaac. You see, I was impatient and thought that God would perhaps say, 'Okay, daughter, you can go ahead. I'll bless you anyway because I know you love Me.' WRONG!!! Yes, He knows that I love Him, but He loves me more. So He had to stop what I was trying to make happen. He gave me the courage to call everything off and believe it or not, I wasn't even embarrassed. *(Okay, maybe I was just a little.)* It was so easy because I knew that I was doing the right thing.

I threw away all my invitations, my bridal party and I got credit slips from the bridal shop, and I sold my ring. My family and I had a party at the reception hall that was reserved and I told that fella to take a hike. He could have the ex-wife and the ex- girlfriend, but he would never have me. WOW!!! What a good feeling it was to finally walk away from this long, dramatic, and tedious ordeal. I never regretted my decision because I learned some valuable life lessons and the importance of waiting on the Lord.

Just a little while longer and that which is promised will come and will not tarry. So don't drawback, just hold on in faith. God loves you, He has better things for you, and He won't forget your labor of love. Don't stagger in your faith. Like Abraham, be fully persuaded that what God has promised, He will do. And if your faith gets a little weak, ask God for strength and He will give you what you need for the journey.

I know you're tired of waiting and you're being tempted to settle for the blessing rather than wait on the promise. But let's look at God's track record:

- The Israelites did enter Canaan. (Joshua 3 and 4)
- Sarah & Abraham did have Isaac. (Genesis 21:1-8)
- Hannah did conceive Samuel. (I Samuel 1:19,20)
- The Hebrew boys did escape the fiery furnace. (Daniel 3:19-30)
- Daniel did come out of the lion's den unharmed. (Daniel 6:16-28)
- Job did receive double for all his trouble. (42:10-17)
- Jesus did rise on the third day. (Matthew 28; Mark 16; Luke 24; John 20; & I Corinthians 15:1-11)
- And we do have access to the Father. (Romans 5:1,2)

So don't faint or lose heart. I know it hurts and feels like God is so far away. But He's in it with you to bring you to a glorious end. Have faith in God! Be fully persuaded that what He promised, He will do. Don't settle for the blessing (Ishmael), but wait on the promise (Isaac). It will surely come to pass!

I don't know where the ex is and I really don't care. I'm just grateful for the experience and the lessons that I learned. I begged God to let us get married and I couldn't understand why He kept saying no. Then one night I had a dream that my then fiancé had a grave dug out just for me. I only escaped because God hid me in a secret place under the shadow of His wings. I couldn't see what God saw. I thought this guy loved me so surely he wouldn't cheat. But cheat is what he did up until the time we were supposed to get married. Why not learn from my experience and save yourself some heartache. If God says no, this is what He means. He's only looking out for your good and He doesn't want you to miss what He has planned for you. I know you're tired of hearing it, but I feel I must say it again:

"Wait on the Lord: be of good courage, and He shall strengthen thine heart. Wait, I say, on the Lord."
Psalms 27:14

DON'T SETTLE FOR ISHMAEL, WAIT ON ISAAC!!!

Do You Know Your Purpose?

"For the Son of Man is come to seek and to save that which was lost."
                                                                    Luke 19:10

"For this purpose the Son of God was manifested that He might destroy the works of the devil."   *I John 3:8*

For the past 10 years and maybe even before that, I have been hearing a lot about the word purpose. Purpose is defined as the reason for which something exists. It's also the original intent of a person or thing and the reason that it was made or created. I believe the whole idea behind purpose is for people to seek the Creator for the reason they were born. This will prevent them from traveling aimlessly through life never reaching their destiny. How sad it is for some people to never find their place in life and ministry hoping that maybe one day they'll stumble upon something that works or strikes their fancy. And it's even more of a pity for an individual to go around the same mountain time and time again never arriving at a specific destination (Deut. 2:3). All of this can be avoided if we would just seek the Lord. He knows why He made each of us and which area of the vineyard should be our focus.

Some subscribe to the belief that if they like something, can do it well, and it's lucrative, then this must be their purpose. As far as relationships, others feel that if two people get along and there's little to no grief, this must be their intended mate. None of these concepts are exactly wrong, but it would be much easier to consult the Lord. He knows exactly which way you should go and who you should choose. Everyone was born with specific ingredients and natural instincts that are necessary to fulfill their task. A brilliant mathematician would probably not pursue a career as an English teacher. More than likely, engineering would be his profession of choice. A skilled painter with no vocal abilities may never audition for the Metropolitan Opera. Instead, his or her focus would be to participate in the latest art show. A born leader may aspire to be president, while an introvert would be more comfortable as a scientist hidden behind a microscope. All of these individuals must tap into their strengths and pursue goals that better suit their abilities. With all of this in mind, I, again, point you back to God. Go to Him for the details of your life. As our Creator, He has the authority to say, "You were made for this" and "You were made for that".

To avoid roaming through life hitting and missing never to reach your destiny, I submit unto to you three passages of scriptures. These scriptures are powerful and necessary for our well-being. If you let them, they will serve as a road map for the journey called life and help you fulfill your purpose. Proverbs 3:5 & 6 says,

"Trust in the Lord with all thine heart and lean not unto thine own understanding. In all thy ways acknowledge him and he shall direct they path."

Then we have Psalms 37:23, which says,

"The steps of a good man are ordered by the Lord: and he delighteth in his way."

If you still need direction, you can specifically request Psalms 119:133, which states,

"Order my steps in thy word: and let not any iniquity have dominion over me."

So you see it is God's will for us to know our purpose and to come to Him for guidance. What I like about God is that He always gives us an example to follow. Jesus was this example who knew exactly what His purpose was. Furthermore, He stopped at nothing until it was fulfilled.

He came to earth with a specific task in mind, which was to redeem man. He wasn't inconvenienced or shocked when He had to come down and dwell among men. Instead, He delighted in doing the Father's will (Psalm 40:8).

In Luke 19:10, He openly declares His purpose. He proclaimed to believers and unbelievers alike that He came to seek and save that which was lost. Then He further concluded in I John 3:8 that He was manifested to destroy the works of the devil.

So you see Jesus knew His purpose. He also wants us to know and fulfill ours. The challenge is that we must go to Him. Sometimes we seek the opinion of others or rely on our own intellect to make sense of it all. But if you want to know the purpose of a thing, don't ask the thing. Ask the one who created it. Like I stated, you don't want to wander aimlessly through life without having a clue where you're going. You need direction. You also need to know that time is too short for you to spend another second in the wrong area of the vineyard. Go to God in prayer so that you can know His voice (I Kings 19:11-13), your purpose (Proverbs 3:6), which way to go and when to change directions (Deuteronomy 2:2, 3). It's that easy! So please seek the Lord so that like Jesus you can know and fulfill your God-given purpose. He doesn't want your time spent on earth to be a complete waste. Instead, He wants you to possess your inheritance and do exactly what you were born to do.

In closing, ask yourself, "Do I know my purpose?" If the answer is no, then you definitely need to seek the Lord. He will make it clear and give you provision for the vision. If the answer is yes, I encourage you to press on and stop at nothing until your mission has been fulfilled.

Make sure you know your purpose and
stop at nothing until it has been fulfilled!

A Simple Equation

Your Confession + Your Reaction = the Manifestation

"For without faith it is impossible to please God: for he that cometh to God must believe that He is and that He is a rewarder of them that diligently seek Him." Hebrews 11:6

"For in blessing I will bless thee and in multiplying I will multiply thy seed as the stars of the heaven and of the sand which is upon the sea shore and thy seed shall possess the gate of his enemies. And in thy seed shall all the nations of the earth be blessed because thou hast obeyed my voice." Genesis 22: 17, 18

In chapter VII, there is a narrative entitled, Time to Reconsider. It examines the Genesis 22 account where Abraham was asked to sacrifice his son. I'd like to revisit this story. To me, it is one of the most intriguing experiences that a person could ever undergo. Because of the outcome, we can all conclude that Abraham truly is the father of faith. Against all odds, he believed God. As a result, his record was approved on high and we have an example by which to live.

The Bible calls Abraham a friend of God and the father of faith (Isaiah 41:8; James 2:23; and Hebrews 11:8-10, 17-19). He rightfully earned these titles because he depicted trust and obedience even in the most adverse situations. What gave Abraham such a stellar record? How did he obtain favor with God? The answers to these questions are simple. His confession and his reaction both pleased the Lord. He said what God wanted him to say and he did what God wanted him to do. This allowed him to be in right standing with God and his promise reaffirmed (Genesis 22:12-18). In like manner, we must confess and react properly in the midst of a test so that we can pass and obtain our inheritance.

Abraham's Confession

Abraham made the right confession in verse 5. Before he went to the mountain, he turned to his men and said,

"I and the lad will go yonder and worship and come again to you."

In other words, as Abraham moved in obedience, he made it clear to his men, "We will be back. We're just going up to worship." He didn't give any further details, but was convinced that Isaac and he would return. This alone pleased the Lord and the outcome was just as Abraham had spoken. He returned with a testimony and Isaac returned unharmed.

Abraham again made the right confession in verse 8. Isaac said, "Dad, I see the fire and the wood. But where is the sacrifice?" Abraham's response was, "My son, God will provide." He knew that God would provide for Himself a lamb for the burnt offering and Isaac would go untouched. This was symbolic within itself. God would provide a lamb on that day. He would also provide a Lamb on Calvary in the form of His Son, Jesus. Jesus would be the ultimate and final sacrifice for the sins of the world and no other offering would be required. Praise God! It's truly amazing how God links everything together and reveals it for our learning.

This is a lesson for us all. When we are being tested and asked of God to do a very peculiar thing, we must say what God wants us to say. We must have the right confession and declare that we're just going up to worship and will be back. Abraham didn't come off the mountain minus a son, but with a testimony declaring that God will provide (22:14). Say what God wants you to say for a victorious end and always have the right confession.

Abraham's Reaction

Abraham also reacted properly when he was told to sacrifice Isaac. His reaction was total obedience, no questions asked. He immediately moved in faith and set out to do what God had commanded. I don't know what was going on in his mind, but I do know that his actions were commendable. Verse 3 says,

"And Abraham rose up early in the morning, and saddled his ass and took two of his young men with him, and Isaac his son, and clave the wood for the burnt offering, and rose up, and went unto the place of which God had told him."

He rose up early in the morning to do what God told him. The Bible doesn't record any conversation between God and Abraham so I assume there was none. God gave the commandment and Abraham moved in obedience. He built the altar, laid Isaac upon it, took the knife and proceeded to slay his only son (verses 9 and 10). WOW! How many of us would have gotten that far. I don't even think we would have made it to the mountain, let alone build the altar. This goes to show that every test is tailor-made for each individual. God knows how to test you and He knows how to test me. Hopefully, we will pass as we learn from Abraham's example. Have the right reaction, which is total obedience.

The Manifestation

This account ends just the way Abraham spoke it. Isaac and he did return and God did provide a lamb. In midair, the angel of the Lord told Abraham to stop and do his son no harm. He proved that he feared God and was willing to give up that which was most important to him (verse 12). A ram was provided (verse 13), God reaffirmed His promise (verses 16-18), and Abraham gave that place a name (verse 14). Jehovah-Jireh it was called because God did provide and He did see to everything working out in Abraham and Isaac's favor.

What a powerful story. In response to our greatest test, we must be willing to go beyond human reason. We must say what God wants us to say and do what God wants us to do. If we apply this simple equation, the outcome will be far greater than what we could ever perceive.

Your Confession + Your Reaction =

the Manifestation

"Table for one, please, non-smoking!"

The following is a fictional account of a woman's desire to find Mr. Right. Her challenges are the inner demons of closed-mindedness and being too judgmental. Can her best friend help her see the light or will she continue to be imprisoned by her own preconceived notions? Let's see as we examine some common issues familiar to us all.

Childhood Dreams

When Cindy was a little girl, she often dreamt of walking down the aisle of a huge crowded church. It wasn't just any aisle, but it was the one that led to her Prince Charming waiting patiently at the altar. In these dreams, Cindy was always adorned in a flowing white gown with a train that never ended. A sheer veil draped over her camel-colored face, yet it did not hide the brilliant smile that enhanced her jovial countenance. The wedding party consisted of nothing but true friends and it was evident that this was a match made in heaven. Cindy looked forward to these nocturnal adventures because she usually had them at least three nights a week. Even though she was only 12, her mom often encouraged her that one day she would meet Mr. Right. And with love, hard work, and determination, it is possible live happily ever after.

There was nothing wrong with these dreams. In fact, every girl has them and looks forward to the day when she can say, "I do." The problem was that 18 years later, at age 30, Cindy was still dreaming. She was still single, had no children, and yet waiting for marital bliss to come her way.

Five years later, at age 35, she felt pressure from her church, family, and even some friends. They were all baffled, along with Cindy, and the question remained, "Will Mr. Right ever come?"

Cindy was usually okay with her marital status. She was engaged once before and had some wonderful dates every now and then. She had a great job and owned a classy brownstone in New York. At present, she is pursuing her doctorate in education and her travels have extended throughout America, Europe and even the Caribbean Islands. She has a wonderful array of friends and her family is always supportive of her decisions. In August of this year she celebrated her 40th birthday and everyone agreed that each day would get better and brighter. Forty wasn't the end, but the beginning of a whole new chapter in her life. With all of this going in her favor, she sometimes still had a void. Luckily, it wasn't enough to prevent her from having a happy and fulfilling life. She was determined to live even if she was single.

Dinner and a Movie

Everything was going smoothly, but something traumatic happened to Cindy one cool October night. She had an awakening experience, something that would change the course of her life forever. On her way home from work, she decided to go to dinner and a movie. Not having a date never stopped Cindy because she had the whole world at her disposal. When she walked into the restaurant, the host came towards her. As usual, she said to him, "Table for one, please, non-smoking."

Even though she had said these words many times before, there was something different about tonight. Each syllable was so audible that they sounded like thunder rolling from her lips. It felt as if the words came from her belly and bellowed from her mouth like an erupting volcano. She was convinced that everyone in the restaurant, including the cook, heard her ask for a table for one. It was a Friday night, she was alone, and there was no one by her side. Half-frozen, she continued what seemed like a long journey to her table. Cindy followed the host and sat down slowly in utter disillusion.

"TABLE FOR ONE, PLEASE, NON-SMOKING. TABLE FOR ONE, PLEASE, NON-SMOKING. TABLE FOR ONE, PLEASE, NON-SMOKING..." sounded like a drum beat pounding in her head. And it would not come to an end.

Cindy was tired of asking for a table for one, non-smoking. When would she be able to request a table for two and the other person not be one of her girlfriends? She couldn't understand it. She was beautiful, successful, passionate, and fun. She never had a problem meeting people, but Mr. Right still hadn't come her way. She began to feel torn inside, but didn't want it to show on her face. She carefully perused the restaurant and it seemed like everyone was a couple except her. She couldn't take it because it was all too painful to bear. While conflicting thoughts bounced around her head, she could hear her biological clock going, "tick, tock, tick, tock", and it wouldn't stop. Cindy couldn't sit still. Pretending to have an emergency, she gave the waiter a brief explanation and immediately vacated the premises. She ran for her car because at the time, it was her only place of refuge. Single, no man, no children ...Single, no man, no children ...Single, no man, no children ...danced in her brain like rain drops against a cement wall. What would she do? Where could she go? When will it end? These questions and more demanded an immediate response for which she could not give. So she left wondering what would be her next move.

Best Friend, Rachel

When Cindy got into her car, she called her best friend, Rachel. Forsaking a formal greeting, she yelled, "Rachel, I need help! I can't believe it. I'm 40 with no man and no children. What on earth is going on? Furthermore, I'm tired of asking for a, table for one, please, non-smoking!"

Hearing the despair in her voice, Rachel immediately told Cindy to come over. Rachel knew that this was no light thing because her friend was a person that usually kept her composure. When Cindy arrived at Rachel's door, no words were exchanged. She just collapsed into Rachel's arms, sobbing unceasingly, trying to make sense of it all. Cindy fumbled her way into the living room and they sat on the couch quiet for about 15 minutes. It wasn't time to talk. Cindy needed a chance to gather her thoughts. Being the kind of friend that she was, Rachel knew that silence was sufficient until someone was ready to share. Cindy had confidence in her friend and knew, like so many times before, she would make everything better.

Rachel, 42, was recently married. This was her second marriage and she often encouraged Cindy to hang in there. "When you least expect it, he will come", is what she often said and these words never failed to ignite hope in her shattered heart. Rachel knew that it was time to talk so she broke the silence with some friendly advice. A fancy introduction wasn't necessary because Rachel knew exactly what her friend needed. Cindy knew that Rachel loved her so she was open to receive every word. Rachel knew that her friend had a rigid upbringing and this sometimes hindered her from having a meaningful relationship. Men were often intimidated by Cindy, but with some careful grooming and smoothing of the rough edges, this could all change.

Rachel advised Cindy to try new things and be open to different kinds of people. Don't settle for second best, but at the same time don't have so many restrictions. Rachel reminded Cindy about Rick. Rick was a lovely young man that Rachel introduced her to sometime ago. Rachel tried her best to hook them up, but Cindy wouldn't budge. Rick didn't come wrapped the way she wanted so she totally negated the possibility.

Rick had a lucrative job, but wasn't exactly polished. He owned a fancy car, but was still renting. He went to church on Sundays, but his dedication to God was a bit inconsistent during the week. Rachel saw potential, but Cindy couldn't see past the earrings and braids that crowned his head. She preferred a clean-cut shaven man and felt that earrings should be worn only by the female gender.

Cindy agreed that she never gave Rick a chance even though he was obviously interested. But this October night, the same night that she uttered, "Table for one, please, non-smoking", she was open for just about anything within reason. It was still early, so Rachel decided to give Rick a call. After a brief conversation, he was elated to know that Cindy wanted to see him again. He knew that their first encounter wasn't too successful, but he was willing to give it another try.

Rachel handed her friend the phone and after a few words, Cindy and Rick decided to go out the following evening. Cindy's tears were now replaced with hope and she was grateful for Rachel coming to her rescue once again. Rachel advised her friend to be open. Don't settle, but be open. Change is a good thing and variety is the spice of life.

Maintain your values and don't evict your standards. But don't let a "closed mind" make you miss an obvious blessing. Cindy received every word and saw this entire ordeal as nothing less than divine intervention. Earlier that evening her world seemed to be caving in. Now Cindy was excited and with great expectation looking forward to her date with Rick. This was the beginning of a new day!

The Date

The time finally arrived for Cindy and Rick to enjoy an evening together. As planned, she arrived at Leo's, a fine Italian restaurant in the city, before he did. When the host came to greet her before he could even ask she blurted out, "Table for two, please, non-smoking!" Oh, my God! This can't be real. This can't be true. Did Cindy hear what she thought she heard? She actually said table for two and the other party wasn't a girlfriend. To the host, these were just mere words that he heard time and time again. To Cindy this was a public declaration that she had a date and would soon be like the others at a *tables pour deux*. Yes, yes, she said it, "Table for two, please, non-smoking!" And she couldn't wait to see what the rest of the night had in store.

Cindy's eyes danced around the restaurant. She would soon be like the rest: a couple, a pair, a twosome. It was special, it was charming, and felt different from all the rest. The host helped her with her chair and told her how nice she looked. She accepted the compliment and knew within her heart that this would be a night to remember.

She sat patiently in her fitted red dress that accented her voluptuous shape. The black stilettos made her legs look bigger than usual and the light make-up complimented her smooth skin. She couldn't wait to see who could possibly be the One. After a year since she had seen Rick, she had an inclination that she wouldn't be disappointed. Although not verbatim, Cindy rehearsed in her mind everything that Rachel told her: Be open. Don't have so many restrictions. Maintain your values. Welcome variety. Don't miss an obvious blessing. "O.K., got it", she thought. Trying not to perspire, the anticipation made it difficult. She gently rose from her chair and glided into the ladies room. Taking a few deep breaths, she powdered her nose and applied a fresh layer of lipstick. She wanted everything to be perfect and after looking in the mirror she was pleased with what she saw. Without hesitation, she strolled back to her seat to await the entrance of her stallion.

Surprise!

After a few minutes went by Cindy looked up. Her face nearly dropped to the floor. She hoped that her mouth wasn't hanging open because she was totally stunned beyond belief. It felt like her heart missed a few beats so she immediately tried to regain her composure. It was Rick! If it weren't for his signal dark eyebrows and dimpled smile, he would have been totally unrecognizable. He was so polished that Cindy was afraid to touch him. His skin was so smooth, that he looked like a newly waxed car. His clothes carefully covered his muscular body and his braids were replaced by a neat haircut. She discretely looked for the earrings that, as she remembered, hung from both ears. Instead she saw none. Only a modest gold chain decorated his chest. Rick was also pleased with what he saw. He broke the silence with a well thought out compliment. After wishing her a happy belated birthday, he gently handed her a single red rose. He finally took his seat and they equally gazed into each other's eyes. Neither one felt forced to speak. Instead they captured the moment by inhaling the aroma of each other's presence.

Rick knew that Cindy had reservations about him the last time they met. Luckily he wasn't at all offended. In fact, he assured her that he exchanged most of his youthful ways for those more compatible to a 40 year old. (Yes, they were the same age). He had just moved into his newly purchased 3-BR home and his church attendance now included weekdays. Even with a recent promotion on his job, there was still a void in his life. Rick had dated off and on, but no one really struck his fancy. He never forgot Cindy, but thought all was lost since their meeting a year ago wasn't too successful.

They caught up on old times and shared their regrets about never taking time to get to know each other. They were so grateful for the reconnect and agreed that Rachel was a brilliant friend. Could this be it? Could this be the One? Cindy asked herself these questions and Rick thought the same things, too.

Cindy felt it necessary to apologize for not being too friendly the last time they met. She knew she could be judgmental at times, but didn't want to settle after waiting so long for the right one. Rick assured her that he didn't think less of her and it served as a wake up call for him. At 39, he realized that it was time for him to make some changes. This was the only way he could attract a lady and someone he wouldn't mind bringing home to Mom. He thanked Cindy for being honest because it gave him something to strive for. They continued to bask in each other's presence and purposely prolonged their meal. Neither one wanted to leave, but wished this moment would last forever. It was everything they had hoped for.

Following dessert they prepared to leave. Each agreed to see each other again and without hesitation exchanged phone numbers. After a couple of laps in a nearby park the wind grew brisk. So they decided to get back into their cars. Rick insisted on following Cindy home to make sure she got in safely and she agreed. After parking behind her, he got out of his car and lifted her from hers. He walked Cindy to her front door and showered her with repeated warm kisses and a gentle round of hugs. She tried not to be distracted by his protruding muscles, but this was ABSOLUTELY impossible. It was clear to Cindy that Rick took pride in his body. His commitment to physical fitness is a quality that she soon learned to admire.

Although it was hard for them to say good-bye, they managed to float to their separate destinations. Had it not been for the wind, Cindy would have still been standing there frozen as Rick's car disappeared down the street. Reluctantly, she went inside and, like a dove, gently slid into her favorite chair. It took a while for her to come back to earth. And when she did, thoughts of the evening made her drift back into oblivion. Time seemed to stand still and her heart was overwhelmed with joy. Could Rick be the one that she had been waiting for? Was her search for Mr. Right finally over? She was convinced that something substantial had taken place and she wasn't about to overlook this obvious blessing.

<u>Thankful</u>

After gaining some strength, Cindy called Rachel. At first she was lost for words. Then she tried her best to describe the wonderful evening Rick and she enjoyed. Cindy thanked her friend for the hook-up, words of wisdom, and bailing her out once again. Rachel reminded Cindy to be open, have standards, and don't miss an obvious blessing. Cindy assured Rachel that she did exactly what she advised. The reconnect was a success and the beginning of something new. They hung up and Rachel knew in her heart that something special had taken place for her friend.

As Cindy sat on her couch, her childhood dreams came back to her. She saw the huge crowded church, long aisle, and Prince Charming waiting at the altar. The flowing white dress, never ending train, and sheer veil that covered her face also resurfaced. By now her dreams included a sparkling diamond ring and romantic honeymoon. A horse and carriage was the mode of transportation and her fantasies seemed more of a reality. Her mother's words even came back to her. She would meet Mr. Right. And with love, hard work, and determination, it is possible to live happily ever after.

Tuesday at noon would be their next date. Again, Rick chose the place and on purpose Cindy decided to arrive early. She wanted the pleasure of saying, "Table for two, please, non-smoking", knowing that the other person would NOT be a female friend. Wow! This certainly was a new day. Whoever said it was right. Life does begin at forty!

What's the Message?

Did you enjoy this story? I hope so because I really enjoyed writing it. There's nothing wrong with a childhood dream, especially when it comes true. More importantly, let's talk about what we learned. Simply put, so often we judge a book by its cover. We don't get to know a person or fully assess a situation before we draw conclusions. We must allow ourselves to go beneath the surface and discover the underlying truth so we won't be deceived or overlook an obvious blessing. The Bible says,

"Therefore judge nothing before the time…"
I Corinthians 4:5

It also says,

"Better is the end of a thing than the beginning thereof: and the patient in spirit is better than the proud in spirit."
Ecclesiastes 7:8

What if God had judged you like Cindy judged Rick? What if God chose not to give you a second chance? What if you didn't have Jesus as your Mediator to plead your case before the Father? Like Rachel defended Rick God will always defend you. Just make sure you give others this same privilege.

Fortunately, Cindy was smart enough to listen to the wise counsel of her friend. This leads to another point. Be humble enough to accept good advice because there is always someone who knows more than you. Proverbs 19:20 says,

"Hear counsel, and receive instruction, that thou mayest be wise in thy latter end."

Cindy stepped outside the box, gave Rick another chance, and maybe she will finally say, "I do." We can't always go by what we see the first time because what we see is usually a work in progress. You just have to stick around for the finished product, which hopefully won't take too long (smile). God portrayed this very thing when He sent the prophet Samuel to anoint David (see I Samuel 16:1-13). Samuel thought that God would choose one of Jesse's other sons to be king, not David. All of his other sons seemingly fit the physical requirements of a king. Yet according to God they didn't have the right heart. Instead God chose David: a young ruddy boy who was good-looking and qualified for the anointing (I Samuel 16:12). You see, God knew his heart. He knew that David had a heart for praise, worship, and service to the Lord. David was also an excellent warrior, a necessary characteristic because kings usually engaged in battle. And he respected leadership. God went past the outward appearance to qualities that are far more essential. This is why David was chosen. Let's consider the following,

"...For the Lord seeth not as man seeth; for man looketh on the outward appearance, but the Lord looketh on the heart." I Samuel 16:7

Aren't you glad that God goes beyond what can be seen with the natural eye? He knows the intent of the heart and judges us according to His love. Yes, love is the criteria by which God bases His decisions. Also, He looks pass our faults and sees our potential. David had potential. In our story, Rick had potential. And you know what? So do you. Let's glory in this and God's ability to shower His grace upon every individual.

God has given us spiritual discernment and perception. These qualities allow us to see the good, the bad, and the ugly in every situation. Sometimes we miss the signals whether it's red, green, or yellow and make a bad choice. But God allows us to recover and gives us another opportunity to try it again. Discernment also allows you to know how far to go in a relationship. Some relationships are extremely lethal and deadly to your well-being. In this case you need to let them go. On the other hand, some relationships are vital and necessary for your life. These are the ones that you should cultivate and retain. Trust your God-given instincts. You have had enough experiences in addition to plain old common sense to make the right choices. And if you do get stuck, don't forget to talk to God and a trusted friend. Between the two, you'll come out all right! Also, there's enough Word inside of you to help you operate in wisdom. So don't be afraid to step out. Your inner alarm will go off before you make a shipwreck. I promise you, God has your back so don't be afraid to live.

Judge nothing before its time, take heed to wise counsel, and trust your instincts. I'm not telling you to lower your standards. I'm just advising you to be open to sudden and unexpected moves of God. He's not going to always do things the same way. Therefore, you must be sensitive to Him and follow His lead.

Again, judge nothing before its time. People, situations, and even you can change. Don't totally negate something or someone because the appearance is not ideal. Give it another try because it may be better the second time around. Ask Cindy. God puts people and situations in your path for a reason. Again, follow His lead. I promise He will reveal the conclusion of the whole matter at the proper time.

Your table for one can turn into a table for two. Trust God in all things and don't be afraid to bust a move! He has your back.

Peace!

"Do I have to be a size 6?"

In total frustration, I believe some women have really asked themselves this question. There is so much pressure from society to lose weight and the fashion industry, as usual, is obsessed with body image. Even the church has subscribed to the ideology that thin is in. This leaves many women disenchanted with nowhere to go for solace and comfort. Furthermore, if you let magazines determine your identity, you'll really be up a creek. You'll be forced to engage in a weight loss regiment that is expected to yield immediate results. If you fail, you will be frowned upon and maybe even sink into a deep depression. With all of this in mind, I think there needs to be a discussion. Let's talk about it and hopefully you'll feel better when the conversation is over.

I truly believe that the motive for losing weight should be to achieve good health. It is not healthy or physically advantageous to be overweight. Excess fat can clog arteries, cause high blood pressure and make you extremely lethargic. To be honest, extra pounds really don't look right. But if you feel comfortable and are not suffering any apparent health risks, then by all means, be content with who you are.

I, for one, know that my weight fluctuates. Sometimes it baffles me how I can fit a blouse one week, and when I try to button it the following week I'm faced with much difficulty. Then I try the same blouse on a third time having much success. I'm a person, because of slow metabolism and heredity, who has to exercise and eat right. If I don't, the pounds will bulge in my mid-section and also give me the appearance of having two chins. (DON'T LAUGH!) Do I always do what I'm supposed to do as far as eating right and exercising? No. However, I do my best sometimes to much avail and other times to much dismay. Progress is apparent, but sometimes it seems like the extra weight is glued to my body with an everlasting adhesive. And if I'm having a "chubby" day I don't want to hear from others, "Are you putting on weight?" What I want to say in the most sarcastic tone possible is, "Are you the same size you were when you were 20? Then don't expect me to be." Usually, the person asking the question is far bigger than me, but he or she feels qualified to make comments about my appearance. To this person I say, "Shut-up!" for lack of a better word. If I need assistance in this weight game, then I'll ask. The pressure is on to be a certain size from society and even the church. So my answer to, "Do I have to be a size 6?" is an emphatic, "NO!" I just have to be healthy.

Again, excess weight is unhealthy. So when you diet and exercise, make sure your motives are right. Make sure you're doing it for yourself with the purpose of being physically fit in addition to looking good. Don't let people pressure you. Don't let society make you feel like you have to look like Beyonce. Yes, she's gorgeous and her shape is something to be desired, but she works at it. She works out religiously and has frequent sessions with a personal trainer. So you can't be mad at her; just do what's best for you. You may not be able to afford a personal trainer, membership to a gym or stick to a complicated diet. So what I suggest is that you make some small yet definite changes. Visit your doctor, avoid fatty and fried foods, don't lie down after eating a hearty meal and engage in some form of activity. Your goal and motive is to be healthy, physically wealthy, and wise, not to please others.

If you're battling with depression and anger because of your weight you must come to one conclusion: This is nothing but the devil. He's feeding you garbage and negative thoughts about you. You are beautiful and you are handsome. So don't let Satan steal, kill, and destroy what God has strategically put in place (John 10:10). He wants to steal your joy. He wants to kill your confidence. And he wants to destroy your concept of self-worth. Don't let him do it because he is a liar! On the other hand, Jesus came so that you can have life and have it more abundantly (John 10:10). He loves you and desires every part of you whether you're a size 6 or a size 20. Why? Because He made us in His image and like the old saying goes, "God doesn't make junk!"

You are fearfully and wonderfully made (Psalms 139:14). This means that you have potential, value, and uniqueness that no one else can duplicate. Also, you are more than a conqueror (Romans 8:37) and greater is He that is in you than he that is in the world (I John 4:4). Again, I stress that any weight lose regiment should be for health purposes and YOUR desire to look a certain way. Let's face it; a figure 8 does look better than a figure 20. In spite of this, lose weight because YOU want to and not because of pressure from others. You are beautiful, you are unique, and God loves you for who you are: His trophy and prize.

Leah had an interesting dilemma as we see in Genesis 29:17 and 18. Jacob, her husband, didn't love her like he loved Rachel his other wife. Why? Because she wasn't too pleasing to the eye. In addition to this, Leah thought by having Jacob's baby he would love her despite what she looked like (29:32). So many young girls and older ones, too, make this same mistake. They feel that having a man's baby is a way to trap him and gain his love. To their dismay, the guy gets up and leaves them to raise the baby alone. Their mission was not accomplished. Leah battled with low self-esteem and a desire to be accepted. Even though these are legitimate feelings, her method did her more harm than good. I don't think she ever really realized her self-worth, but was more concerned with pleasing her man.

Leah had many children trying to get Jacob to love her. She conceived Reuben, Simeon, Levi, and then Judah. She stopped bearing for a season and chose rather to praise God. She declared in Genesis 29:35, "Now will I praise the Lord." Yes, she stopped bearing for a season, but went on to give

Jacob two more sons, Issachar and Zebulum, and a daughter, Dinah. Unfortunately, she wasn't quite satisfied with just praising the Lord. There was still an underlying desire to please Jacob. With six sons and one daughter, we can conclude that she was fruitful even if Jacob didn't think she was beautiful. She gave birth just like you can. You are fruitful and able to produce despite the pressures you feel to look a certain way or be a certain size. Love yourself, acknowledge your self-worth and don't let the enemy paralyze you with low self-esteem. Don't do things to try to please people. Furthermore, women, don't have a man's baby thinking this is the way to get him to love you. Love yourself! Celebrate yourself! Worship God for who and how He made you. Lose the weight because you want to and don't let pressures from others control you. Words from others can lead to depression, resentment, and eating disorders like bulimia and anorexia. So be smart and consider my way. I'm watching my weight and what I eat because I want to, not because of pressures from someone else. If someone is going to love me, they must love me for who I am, despite the size of my package. Like I said, realistically speaking, a figure 8 does look better than a figure 20. But whatever you do, do it for you, not to satisfy others.

Do you have to be a size 6? NO!!! JUST…

- Love yourself!
- Realize that you are fearfully and wonderfully made.
- Know that you have the greater One on the inside.
- Lose weight for health reasons and because YOU want to, not because others want you to.
- Believe that you are unique and no one else can duplicate what you have to offer.

Acknowledge your worth and, like Leah, go ahead and produce in Jesus' Name!

Your Responsibility

It's important to recognize your responsibility when it comes to certain issues in life. All the weight can't be put on God because He is not going to do everything. In order for you to live a fruitful life, obedience and works must accompany your faith. You must make a conscious effort to work your harvest so that you can inherit your promise.

With this in mind, I submit unto you the task of doing your part when it comes to the following areas: salvation, human relationships, sanctification, finances, and faith. God and you would make a wonderful team. But you can't sit idle expecting Him to play all the positions. You must get off the bench, get into place, and be determined to play until you win.

Salvation

In reference to salvation, you must accept your responsibility by asking the right questions. Whether it's verbally or an utterance of the heart, personal accountability will help determine your spiritual state. Let's consider the Philippian jailor in Acts 16:30 and 31. His conversion was the result of God's mercy, his ability, and willingness to ask the right question. If you read the scriptures, you will see what I mean. He didn't say, "God what must YOU do in order for me to be saved?" Instead, he said, "Sirs, what must I do to be saved?" He realized that there was something he had to do. Jesus had already done His part by dying on the cross and rising on the third day. Now he had to get his will involved in order to get to the next step.

Paul and Silas were more than happy to give the Philippian jailor further instructions. They simply told him to believe on the Lord Jesus Christ. As a result, his family and he would be saved. The jailor and his house received the Lord, were baptized, and rejoiced because of their new position in God (verses 32-34).

In John 3, we are introduced to Nicodemus. Nicodemus was a prominent ruler of the Jews who had enough humility to acknowledge his own spiritual lack. Although a Pharisee, someone learned in the Law, he needed a better understanding of kingdom principles and the spiritual procedure of being born again. Like the Philippian jailor, Nicodemus asked the right questions according to his understanding. He said to Jesus,

"How can a man be born when he is old? Can he enter the second time into his mother's womb, and be born?" (Verse 4)

Of course not! Jesus was talking about a spiritual rebirth. Yet He didn't brush him off as some imbecile. On the contrary, He took the time to explain what Nicodemus clearly didn't understand. Jesus, moved by this man's humility and innocence, explained the experience of a spiritual rebirth given to those who believe. Jesus also protected this man's identity. Nicodemus came to Jesus by night because he didn't want to be found out by the other Jewish leaders. If this would have happened, he would have been excommunicated and maybe even killed. Just like today, Jewish leaders of that time denied Jesus and to accept Him was considered blasphemous. Yet Nicodemus took a chance by seeking Jesus at night. And Jesus gave him what he needed: an opportunity to be saved.

The Philippian jailor and Nicodemus asked the right questions and accepted their responsibility in the plan of salvation. God extended His love to them along with the free gift of eternal life. You, too, can have this same privilege. Come to God with a willing heart and you will be saved. He will in no wise cast you out, but extends an open invitation for you to come and dine with Him (Revelation 3:20). Accept your responsibility in the plan of salvation. Like these two Bible characters, ask the right questions, confess Jesus as Lord, and you will be saved. For further enlightenment, please read John 3:1-21; 6:37; Acts 16:31; and Romans 10:9-13. RECEIVE JESUS TODAY AND THE FREE GIFT OF ETERNAL LIFE!

Human Relationships

This is one of my favorite topics because I value true friendships and my ability to get along with others. I am no relationship guru, but I will share what I know.

First and foremost, you need other people. As the old saying goes, "No man is an island and no man stands alone." Also, there is no "I" in teamwork. Therefore, you need other people in order to exist and get the job done.

An important point comes from Solomon in Eccl. 4: 9-12. This scripture points out that two are better than one. Why? If one falls, the other can pick him up. Logically speaking, if you fall and no one is around you will have an extremely difficult time getting up. Therefore, you can't have a solo act all the time or try to exist in isolation. This is foolish! You must establish positive and productive relationships with someone other than yourself. In order to do this, it's imperative that you tear down your walls of separation and let other people in.

The Bible also makes it very clear that YOU must love your neighbor like you love yourself (Mark 12:31; Luke 19:18; and Romans 13:9). In other words, you must value others the same way that you value *you*. This is the only way that relationships can be established and maintained. Love self and others so that you won't be alone.

Your relationship with others is also determined by your friendliness. To have friends you must first show yourself friendly (Proverbs 18:24). Always have a warm spirit and create a congenial atmosphere so that others won't mind being in your presence.

Also, be gentle, remember that a soft answer turns away wrath, and always be willing to forgive (II Timothy 2:24; Proverbs 15:1; Ephesians 4:32). Forgiveness is so essential that I must include the scripture as it is written,

"And be ye kind one to another, tenderhearted, forgiving one another, even as God for Christ's sake hath forgiven you." Ephesians 4:32

Forgive others just like Christ forgave you. Holding a grudge will benefit no one, especially you. So let it go. Also, don't be so quick to sever a relationship just because another person and you are experiencing some difficulties at the moment. Walk away, take some time off from each other and be willing to reunite as the Lord leads. Sometimes God will tell you to leave it alone. Other times He will tell you to give it another try. Whatever the case, be open and responsive to the leading of the Holy Ghost. Accept your responsibility in establishing and maintaining positive human relationships because it's foolish to try to exist alone.

Sanctification

Without sounding legalistic or doctrinal, I'll briefly discuss sanctification and your responsibility therein. Sanctification is the process by which the Holy Spirit cleanses and purifies us making us fit for the Master's use. I believe that it begins when a person gets saved and continues until Jesus comes. Sanctification also involves a person's will and cooperation with the Holy Ghost so that a complete work can be done. When I was coming up, I saw sanctification as clothes and a list of, Dos and Don'ts. Now I see it as a partnership between a person and the Holy Spirit. In love, God tells us what to put on and what to put off (Colossians 3:1-17). In love, we simply obey. In doing so, we are becoming more like Him so that we can be lights in this dark world. It's not so much the outer appearance, even though this is a part of it. But it encompasses a person's heart and lifestyle dedicated to God for His will, purpose, and glory (I Peter 3:15; 1:15).

Leviticus 10:10 says that YOU must put a difference between holy and unholy, clean and unclean.
I Thessalonians 5: 22-24 declares that YOU must abstain from all appearance of evil. Do all that you can do in order to honor God with your life and He will come in and do the rest. Don't put all the responsibility on Him to sanctify YOU. Set yourself aside, refrain from that which displeases Him, and glorify God with your spirit, soul, body, and lifestyle.

How did I do? Does this sound like a legal document of holiness? I hope not. I just want you to accept the importance of this issue. Sanctification is not preached as often as it was when I was coming up. Leaders don't want to offend the flock and people are determined to do what they want. But this does not exclude me from expressing a biblical truth. In love, I conclude with this brief statement. God wants us to mimic Him (I Peter 1:16). He wants us to be holy (set aside and sanctified) in all manner of living. Therefore, we must cooperate with the Holy Spirit and honor God with our entire state of being. He's here to assist in the process so that we won't have to do it alone. Work in agreement with the Holy Spirit. God will be pleased and you will be made the better for it. Be blessed!

Finances

This is a sticky subject because many of us, especially the saints, have very poor money management skills. We live above our means, don't save, and fail to make provisions for the future. Don't put everything on God and when you do foolish things expect Him to bail you out. Be wise with your money, give Him His ten percent (Malachi 3:10-12), and properly manage the rest. Here are some scriptures and advice to help you obtain financial victory:

- Consider the ant. In other words, go to work *Lazy* and save so that poverty won't be your portion (Proverbs 6:6-11).
- God has given you the power and strength to make wealth (Deuteronomy 8:18). Your responsibility is to go out and get it because wealth will not miraculously land in your lap.
- Financial victory is also the result of being a giver. Give and people will give back to you. How? Pressed down, shaken together, running over, back in good measure will men give unto your bosom (Luke 6:38). Also, the liberal soul will be made fat (Proverbs 11:25). If you keep your hands closed, nothing will go out and nothing will come in. Learn how to give to others because this is a sure way to receive.
- Pay your tithes and offering (Malachi 3:8-12). Give God His 10% and be a good steward over the 90% that belongs to you. Save, invest, give, and live. This is the Bible way.

There is a biblical principle called seedtime and harvest (Genesis 8:22). The earth reproduces that which is planted and this cycle continues year round. This principle can also be evident in your life. The reciprocity of sowing and reaping, planting and harvesting are essential. So make sure you are planting in good ground so that you will receive a harvest of blessings. A God-ordained ministry is good ground. The Atlantic City casinos are not. Legal investments are good ground. Crooked schemes are not. A retirement plan and your children's college education are good ground.

Just living for today is not. A financial plan and budgeting are good ground. Frivolous spending and riotous living are not. Make better financial choices so that God can say,

"Well done, thou good and faithful servant: thou hast been faithful over a few things, I will make thee ruler over many things: enter thou into the joy of the Lord." Matthew 25:23.

Faith

You probably know by now that Abraham is one of my favorite people. He exemplified faith when there was absolutely, positively no evidence of manifestation. Through faith and the work of obedience, he received the promise (Isaac) and obtained a good report from the Lord.

Briefly stated, works must accompany your faith. According to James 2:26, without works your faith is DEAD. You can pray all you want. You can fast all you want. You can quote scriptures all you want. You can name it and claim it all you want. But if you don't get up and work your harvest you will have a DIM outcome. If you refuse to cooperate with this principle, your results will be net zero.

Do all that you can do in order to bring things to past in your life. For instance, if you believe God for healing, you must obey the doctor's orders. Eat right and exercise so that you can enjoy good health. If you believe God for a job, have faith as well as actively look for one. Get the proper training and education so that you can get the career of your choice. If you believe God for victory in any situation, do all that you can do within your power and He will do the rest. Asking, seeking, and knocking denote a continual process (Matthew 7:7-11). Therefore, you can't give up at your first attempt. Have faith in addition to being persistent. Combine works with your faith and you will get an optimum return.

Psalms 24:1 says, "The Earth is the Lord's, and the fullness thereof; the world, and they that dwell therein." Since you belong to God and everything belongs to Him, you are working with a clear advantage. The world is at your disposal so GO OUT AND GET IT! Put some works behind your faith and you will receive a great reward.

In conclusion, let's take advantage of all that God has made available for His people. Make no more excuses and don't expect Him to do everything. Do your part in the areas of salvation, human relationships, sanctification, finances, and faith and God will do the rest. Whatever He started in you, He will complete it (Philippians 1:6). Just don't forget to do your part! Open doors of opportunities have been set before you (Revelation 3:8). Now go out and get it!

Final Words

What a privilege it has been to share my thoughts with you. I pray that it was equally a pleasure for you to have read them. One of the goals of this project was to inspire and push you to the next dimension in your life. If I can get there, so can you. All you have to do is seek the Lord diligently until He reveals what you were specifically born to do. And stop at nothing until your purpose has been fulfilled.

I know there are some writers, teachers, and other leaders out there who just need someone to steer them along the right path. I hope I did just that. I hope you have been enlightened to the point of seeking God for the role that only YOU can fulfill in His master plan. You may not be a writer, but there is a God-given talent in you that He's waiting for you to tap into. And you know what? You can have more than one. Discover who you are and what you were born to contribute because no one else can do it but you. You are fearfully and wonderfully made, your uniqueness is a heavenly gift, and you need to be revealed and shared by all.

The eye can't say it has no need for the mouth because who will do the talking? The heart can't say that it doesn't need the legs because who will do the walking? Every part of the physical body is needed. If one part is disabled then the other members will have to work harder in order to make up the difference. If you don't do what you were created to do, then someone else will have to work double. You don't want that, now do you? I didn't think so. Be honest with yourself. You know there's more to you than what meets the eye. You just need to become reacquainted with yourself to discover what avenues in life you were meant to travel. I know you think it's too late or you're too old to start something new. Wrong answer! It's never too late. As long as you have breath in your body there's hope, there's time and God is there to give you clarity. I opened this project by telling you that somebody somewhere is waiting to hear your song. Somebody somewhere is waiting for what only you can give. All you have to do is say *yes* and the Lord will fill in the details as you go along.

As a woman, I am a direct descendent of Eve. I was commissioned by God to be a voice of inspiration and I hope I did not fail at my task. Stop at nothing until you have satisfied that which was placed in your care. By doing so, God will be pleased and you will experience the abundant life that He desires for us all (John 10:10; Ephesians 3:20).

Taken from Revelation 3:8, allow me to revisit the poem entitled, *Doors of Opportunities.* I pray that you will take advantage of everything that God has to offer and receive all that He has in store. Like I said before, you belong to God and God belongs to you. This means that you are working with a clear advantage. But you must refuse to settle for mediocrity and aspire to achieve greatness in Him. Go out and get it and stop at nothing until you are an <u>occupant</u> of your promise land. You have visited long enough. Now take up residence and enjoy your land that is flowing with milk and honey. BE BLESSED!!!

Doors of Opportunities

"I know thy works: behold, I have set before thee an open door, and no man can shut it." Revelation 3:8

Open doors of opportunities
Are right before your face
Take advantage of this time
Walk at a steady pace.

Please do not take too long
Or else it'll pass you by
And maybe never come again
So grab it while it's nigh.

The earth contains everything
That you'll ever need
So look to those who have gone
Before you and take heed.

There's no telling just how far
In life you will soar
With a positive attitude
You'll accomplish so much more.

I wish you well and God's speed
As you take your rightful place
Amongst the heroes of our time
Who refused to play it safe.

Don't be afraid to walk on water
Jesus will take your hand
Look to Him in faith believe
And you'll possess the land.

Excuses should from your mouth
Never, ever proceed
Positive confessions are the way
That you will succeed.

Open doors of opportunities
Are right before your face
God is right by your side
To help you win the race.

Now it's time to enjoy
All that you've worked for
So settle down and take your rest
He'll give you so much more.

A teacher by profession, Keshia currently resides in Maplewood, NJ. As a minister in New Brunswick, NJ, it is her distinct mission to encourage and inspire people wherever she goes. Feel free to contact the author with your comments and well-wishes at keshyasp@yahoo.com or Keshia@theribspeaks.com.

You can also order additional copies of this book at www.theribspeaks.com.